nection with the *Creator* comes first

nected with
onoring my
wants

I balance and replenish my energy throughout the day

M MY SOUL FRAGMENTS AND FEEL COMPLETE

ole
ody,
soul

I am worthy of being myself

I deserve to
express my true
Self freely and I do

vious to other people's judgment and trust that
nistake will help me to learn and grow in a safe way

g and taking
myself feels
lly nurturing

I feel worthy,
loved
and accepted,
whether I take action or
allow myself to just be

I KNOW THAT
WHAT I DO AND
WHO I AM
IS ENOUGH AND
GOOD ENOUGH

ctice
love
let go
naturally

I am responsible for my own life, not for others, and live in my highest and best way with respect towards others

I am grateful for everyone and everything in my life, and know that I will always be provided for

I FEEL HOPEFUL,
ange,
PEACE,
EN TO
unlimited possibilities

MW01532795

eintobliss.com

Namaste!

Cut out this page and tape it to your mirror, fridge, o
other place that you will frequently see to remind yo
you ARE worthy of being happy. All the time.

In Divine Friendship & Gratitude,

Anke

PRAISE for *"No Pain, All Gain"*

"Many books promise relief from pain, but very few go beyond the physical components to address the mental, emotional, energetic, and spiritual aspects of healing. This book places those subtle factors at the center of the process—not in an airy-fairy, wishful-thinking way, but by emphasizing practical methods backed by centuries of successful use and a growing body of scientific evidence. Every family should have a copy on a shelf for easy access when needed."

Philip Goldberg
Author of *American Veda* and *The Life of Yogananda*

"If you are alive, pain is inevitable. It's not something we have any choice about. Suffering, however — how we deal with the pain that is inevitable for sentient beings — is something we can do something about. This book asks you to try these ancient remedies and see if and how they can help relieve the suffering that is the birthright of mortals. Anke asks you to pay attention, rather than to believe. To internalize these practical actions in addition to any medical or mental practices that have granted you some relief."

Howard Rheingold
American writer and critic
Taught at Stanford University and UC Berkeley
(digital journalism, virtual communities, social & participatory media)
Research fellow at the *Institute for the Future*
Co-founder of the *Rheingold Learning Network*

"No Pain, All Gain" offers the reader a comprehensive guide for balancing life through a well-integrated composition of the many aspects of Yoga: Raja Yoga (conquering internal nature), Karma Yoga (selfless service), Bhakti Yoga (devotion) and Jnana Yoga (knowledge). Enjoy!"

Ashoka Nalamalapu
Speaker, author, community leader
Host and facilitator of spiritual events

"In the early 1980's, I attended a series of lectures given by my spiritual teacher, Swami Kriyananda, entitled 'Yoga As a Way of Life.' I thought of those lectures often, as I read this book, because of the similar thoroughness of how Anke Banderski , author of "No Pain, All Gain", covers the many aspects of yoga, with such great clarity, and in just one book! Yoga, in all of its different aspects and branches, meets the challenge of being able to help us live our lives well, free from pain, unhappiness, and un-healthiness. In "No Pain All Gain", Anke plays her part very well in clarifying exactly how we can accomplish these very worthy life-goals."

Nayaswami Savitri Simpson
Yoga and Meditation Teacher for over 50 years
Author of *Chakras for Starters*, *The Meaning of Dreaming*, *The Chakras Workbook*, and *The Treta Yuga Trilogy* of *"Spiritual Novels."*

"OMG! This is fantastic!"

Robert Christiansen
Ex-VP of Strategy in the CTO Office at Hewlett Packard Enterprise
Cloud technology leader, motivator, speaker, and innovator
Contributing writer for *CIO magazine*
Editor in Chief for *The Doppler*
Host of the *Motive For Life Podcast*

Anke Bandersski's "No Pain, All Gain" has (a lot of) excellent, powerful, and life-transforming exercises and information."

Joseph (Puru) Selbie
Author of "The Physics of God", "The Yugas", and " Break Through the Limits of the Brain"

No Pain, All Gain

Self-healing for Pain Relief!(C)

7 Encapsulated Keys
To Guide Your Self-healing & Pain Relief

Anke Banderski

No Pain, All Gain

Self-healing for Pain Relief!(c)

Publisher(s): Casey Hughes & Anke Banderski ©

Credits:
Covers and Layout: Casey Hughes
Graphic Designs: Casey Hughes
Editing: Casey Hughes
Photography by Elisabeth Granli (www.ElisabethGranliPhotography.com)

ISBN: 979-8-218-38567-5

Disclaimer:

I HAVE READ, UNDERSTAND and ACCEPT the "Acknowledgment of Risks and Waiver Agreement" found at the back of this book, and intend that it be binding on me, my heirs, executors, administrators and assigns, and if I am accepting on behalf of a minor child, I represent and warrant that I am doing so with the consent and approval of the requisite parent and/or spouse (if any) and I understand that I am acknowledging the risks to said child.

To those in pain, that they may find freedom.

"Even a little practice of this inward science will free you from dire fears and colossal suffering."

Bhagavan Krishna

Table of Contents

Foreword

You *are* ready for this! The journey you have embarked upon, with the book you are now holding, has the potential for life-changing experiences, and a promise of bringing you more joy, more peace, more lasting happiness than you have ever thought possible. That is IF you're ready and willing. So, buckle up and embrace this personal sojourn, vital for a life filled with sustainable health, happiness, peace, and joy. **Afterall, don't you deserve to be happy ALL THE TIME?**

To begin, you must embrace the truth that you are a Divine Being (Spirit) having a human (material) experience! You are far more than a material body. Yes, it's true, you are no less valued in the Universal Collective than the largest galaxy, or the smallest subatomic particle. Each of us has our own unique role to play in this mystery of life. Often hidden, vague, misinterpreted, and misaligned, our role doesn't so much define us as we define it.

Still, you and I live in a time of great turmoil. Our communities across all their specific contextual references, be they familial, academic, religious, financial, athletic, social, or any host of other institutionalized frameworks, have shown a continual decline in their ability to bring us together. To protect us, to heal us, to move us ahead through the turmoil we face each day. Young or old, the statistics on individual depression speak volumes. Individually and collectively, our institutions seem to have forgotten us. Unable to bring us lasting happiness, peace, wellness, and fulfillment. Truth be told, we have forgotten ourselves!

And so we live in fear. Fear of being seen, of NOT being seen, of being ignored, unheard, of being pushed out of our community, our communities. And in doing so, each day we tune our consciousness to the channels of symptomatic relief. We reach for the "bottle", be it prescription or over the counter, alcohol, or "energy" drink.

We long to belong. To be accepted. Without it we cannot survive. We wish only for happiness, and the avoidance of pain. So we ask, "where do we find sustainable wellness today?"

Very recently, I had an experience so illustrative of the current state of our wellness community.

The nurse had just removed the device from my 93-year-old mother's index finger. Writing, head down on her clipboard, I had to ask, "so what are the results?" "98 pulse, 96 blood oxygen" she replied, not bothering to look at me.

Focusing my attention to my mom's doctor standing bedside, I commented "isn't 98 a bit elevated?" Without waiting for a reply, I looked at my mom, her anxiety apparent from having just been rushed by ambulance to this hospital bed. I assured her, a slightly elevated heart rate, given the circumstances, was quite understandable. Still, I knew her "agitated" state of mind, and body, could benefit greatly, from the simplest breath work. Looking her in the eyes I asked, "Mom, would you like to join me in a 2-minute, simple practice of "measured breathing" and enjoy the immediate benefits of relaxation and a lower heart rate?"

Before she had even a moment to answer, her doctor stepped forward and asked her, "would you like me to prescribe medication? It will make you feel better". Horrified, I deflected her directive and asked if I could conduct a quick test, using the finger device the nurse still held. "A simple pranayama can do plenty for my mom right now without any prescription medication. Let me show you, and my mom."

After placing the finger device, my mom and I, holding our gaze with a smile, took 3 deep inhalation breaths followed by complete exhalations. Each while holding our gaze uplifted to the point between the eyebrows, and visualizing health, peace, and happiness. Within 2 minutes the device's LED read-out displayed a dropping series of numbers, finally landing at 83. A 15% drop in her heart rate in under 2 minutes!

The smile alone was priceless as my mother shifted from a state of sad trauma to one of hope. She turned to her doctor and shook her head "no thank you".

Clearly, we live in a society addicted to traditional methods for pain relief. An addiction pandemic in our society. We abdicate our health to our healthcare practitioners without the benefit of full disclosure of the treatments prescribed, the tests made, and the ramifications each has on our quality of life. Or the advancement of our own self-knowledge, critical to understand much about our own bodies, and its capacity for self-healing. So most fly blind, victims of a system growing increasingly out of touch with the basic premise of wellness - that each of us have within us the most powerful healing possibilities, most as yet unrealized. That our bodies, at their very core, were crafted for self-healing.

Yoga, as a system for living, is our salvation as a species. It answers the question, "why are we here?" And "How do we live a perfectly balanced life in harmony with nature and each other?" (make reference to book content re yoga...)

We abdicate everything… learning to our teachers, self-love to our relationships with others, discipline to our parents, wellness to our doctors, and so on.

This book is a wonderful primer for *simple living and high thinking* (quoting my Guru Paramhansa Yogananda). In *"No Pain, All Gain"*, Anke is not attempting to diminish the role traditional wellness practitioners play in the health and well-being of all people and societies (esp. doctors, nurses, pharma companies, etc.). We both share a profound respect for the struggles they too face in bringing forth wellness within a template out of touch with the science, ancient and modern, which now reflects a common understanding. As East and West have slowly found their paths to converge, so have the ancient teachings of the mystics, seers, saints and sages of all religions. The traditional science of materialism IS FINALLY being integrated with the more ancient science of religion. Together they form a more perfect whole!

There is so much more to understand about the state of our bodies, minds, and spirits than these traditional practitioners currently demonstrate a deep understanding and appreciation for. They are locked in the dogma of tradition and lack the necessary institutional support for the basic science for which their individual oaths have been sworn.

But this can, and will, change. Already we are seeing within our leading Universities and Medical Schools, a profound interest in natural healing. In the ancient science of religion as it now informs our most recent advances in material science. We are coming of age to new understandings previously ignored.

Yet it remains a journey of Self Realization. To remember that you are far more than what you have been taught. That only you possess the power for lasting inner happiness.

Within you lies the key. You truly do have the power!

And within this book, we trust you will discover many answers enabling you to embrace your highest nature.

You deserve to be happy… all the time!

Casey Hughes
Ananda Encinitas

Introduction

What do YOU *really* want? Most would answer, "to be happy and free from all suffering". It is a natural desire, and our birth right, to feel good and be happy. Yet, through challenging experiences, many people find themselves angry, frustrated, resentful, sad - far away from feeling good and being happy. Painful emotions eventually block the energy flow in the body and, over time, cause physical pain, illness and disease.

My intention is to elevate people who live in chronic pain, frustration, anger, defeat, and confusion - to a higher vibration of peace. David R. Hawkins' Map of Consciousness shows that each person who lives in the energy of peace can counterbalance 10 million people vibrating in lower frequencies, such as anger, fear, grief, guilt, and shame. This book has the potential of healing 10 million people by the first reader!

So how can YOU turn your life around and be happy **all the time** when you are in serious pain and facing life's struggles? Whether you are standing, sitting, lying down, in a car, on a plane, at your desk, at home, inside, outside… You can practice simple tools explained in this book that will help you to feel better, no matter where you are. Many of the practices described in this book have been practiced for thousands of years. I have experienced great physical, mental, emotional, and spiritual benefits from the practices. Yogananda suggests that there is nothing like direct experience. Practice them, and notice how you feel before and after the practices. They are suggestions. Do what feels uplifting and expansive for you. Be patient and loving with yourself and the practices. You and they will evolve over time.

If you are uncertain about anything in this book I recommend referring to the Bibliography and Glossary at the end of this book. You will find scientific and medical research in the Glossary that provide a grounding basis for many of the practices. Do not get caught up in trying to understand everything with your logical mind, as the mind can only explain a small percentage of what reality is.

Unlock the mystery of inner pain through 7 simple encapsulated keys. In this book, I will guide you to get back on track, to help you to focus on what you want, re-align your mind with your body, spirit and soul, create life force in your body, discover your purpose and live a peaceful, happy and fulfilled life.

All you need is a commitment to feel good and be happy as a regular state of being, not just in a particular situation.

When one is sick or experiencing physical pain, it appears easy to give into medications, alcohol, and other forms of traditional pain relief of lower vibrations. I'm not suggesting all medications are bad, at times they are necessary and helpful. Yet too often, traditional medication proves only to be a quick fix that covers up the symptoms of pain without actually solving the imbalance which caused it.

When I had a cold, I simply didn't feel like making fresh green juice, even though I knew it would help to heal. I did not make one. The next day I committed to feeling better, I made a green juice, rested and felt much better. It takes commitment to want to feel better before we can take beneficial actions. If you feel "down", whether it is emotionally or physically, affirm to yourself "I deserve to feel good!"

Then take the necessary actions towards feeling good. When someone has been sick, anger can be the first emotion that arises, so anger is not always a negative emotion to experience. Anger is often followed by joy.

"Choose happiness. It just feels better."

Dalai Lama

Create a Positive Lifestyle

How do YOU choose to perceive your world?

When you are driving or walking, stopped at a red light, do you get frustrated because you have to wait? See it as a precious opportunity to pause and focus on your breath.

This miracle, breath (or life force), that keeps you alive, enables your thoughts to slowly diminish, your heart to beat more slowly, and you become calmer and more peaceful.

It is in this state of being that you can feel deep gratitude for all that you are. And all that you have. There is something positive, beautiful in every moment, and in every experience. Each moment and situation are a blessing - if we choose to see it that way.

Focus on the beauty in life rather than what's missing, wrong and not working. Life is perfect just the way it is. You are perfect just the way you are. Life is like a river. There are turns and boulders that change the flow of the water, just like obstacles in your life. These may seem to change or block life's flow. Truth is, they are there to guide and strengthen us along our life's path.

"A record of our emotional life is written on our hearts," says cardiologist Sandeep Jauhar, whose work explores the ways emotions impact our hearts - "causing them to CHANGE SHAPE in response to grief or fear, or to literally BREAK due to heartbreak." Just as our hearts change shape in response to painful emotions, we can re-shape our hearts by choosing gratitude, love, joy, and peace.

The more flexible you are and adapt to such challenges, while continuing to focus on how beautiful life really is despite the challenges, the more joy, peace and happiness you will experience.

What is it that you really want? Shift out of being or feeling like a victim into proactively co-creating with your Divine Creator within (God)! Anything is possible. You simply need to be clear about what you want, express it and let your higher power guide you in taking the necessary steps towards it.

***"Stop acting so small.
You are the universe in ecstatic motion."***

Rumi, 13th century sufi mystic

You are your own creator. Prove it to yourself... with three conscious breaths you can easily lower your heart rate. This is just one example of how you can create high quality health and life. Painlessly and instantly!

You may ask "is it selfish to focus on myself and my own happiness, if other people around me are struggling?" This is a great question that David R. Hawkins answers in a powerful way in his book "Power vs Force".

His map of consciousness indicates that a person vibrating in peace counterbalances 10 million individuals vibrating in anger, fear, grief and other frequencies of a lower nature. This shows that your inner peace and happiness is not just important for yourself, but also to uplift humanity!

Feeling good and being happy may seem easier said than done. To a certain extent you can set your intention to feel good and be happy and convince yourself that you are feeling it. At least 80% of what is driving us is subconscious. If you like to be happy, your conscious mind, which accounts for only 20%, wants to convince the subconscious mind, which consists of the remaining 80%, to change.

That's a nice wish, but challenging to achieve in day-to-day life, unless we have specific tools like Meditation, Yoga, and ThetaHealing®, which are all detailed throughout the pages of this book.

Let us begin with some simple steps - **7 Encapsulated Keys to lasting peace, health and happiness.**

I congratulate you for your willingness and readiness to step into your power as a divine being and to live your life to your highest potential.

This takes courage, trust, faith and commitment. All characteristics you will begin to embody as you take this journey with me.

I am honored to guide you along your journey of self-discovery towards a happy, healthy and peaceful You.

In deepest gratitude,

Anke

“I am worthy of God’s love and support.”

The First Key - Intention

Nothing in the universe happens without intention.

"You realize that all along there was something tremendous within you, and you did not know it."

Paramhansa Yogananda

What is your intention at this time?

It may be to feel good and be happy. What does that mean to you personally?

Exercise

1. Drop from your mind into your heart.
2. Breathing through your nose, take five breaths into your heart center.
3. Ask your heart "what do you need at this time?" Allow your heart to respond. **This response* is your intention.**

*If you are not receiving a response from your heart, think about what you would like to bring into your life, and set that as your intention. Your intention may be to let go of physical or emotional pain, be healthy, feel safe in your home and body, trust yourself and others, be successful, prosperous, feel peace or gratitude.

Take this moment to breathe with your intention.

Now journal below and write from your heart, starting with **"I feel good, and I am happy"**. Allow the words to come straight from your heart, rather than your logical mind.

Freely write for 10 minutes, in your own language, without analyzing, judging, or thinking too much about what you're writing.

Journal Here

After 10 minutes, lay down your pen and read what you wrote, without judgment. This can give you a great sense of how you really feel about yourself, how you relate to feeling good and being happy, or the intention you set for yourself, at this time.

Do you believe and feel that you deserve it, even if others around you are struggling? Do you believe it is possible for you to experience it?

This is your time. You deserve to feel good and be happy and it absolutely is possible for you to experience this, no matter what others tell you. **Setting an intention is the first step in manifesting your dreams**. Take some time for yourself now to set your intention. The 4 steps of intention setting below will help you.

Intention Setting

Step 1: Reflect on what it is that you want and write it down with clarity.

____

____

____

____

Step 2: Share your intention with someone you trust who will supportively hold you accountable for your actions towards manifesting your dream.

Step 3: Do something today and every day from now on that will demonstrate your commitment to your intention. Remember that we are human beings, not human doings. If you naturally move through life quickly and are an action person, practicing taking time to be consciously present is a powerful action step.

Step 4a: Acknowledge that you did what you said you were going to do and then move forward to your next action that is in alignment with your intention.

Step 4b: If you did not follow through with your intention, reflect on the reason without beating yourself up. It is helpful to physically take a step back to slip into the observer role in which we can objectively observe the situation, your actions (or non-actions), and be fully present with your thoughts, feelings and the challenge you may have experienced that prevented you from living your intention.

Write down why you didn't follow through and what you will change, so that you will live your intention from now on. It may be changing your mindset or setting time aside for your intention, knowing that you are worthy of it. Love yourself unconditionally no matter what.

Reason why I didn't follow through:

____

____

____

____

What will I change, so that I will follow through from now on:

____

____

____

____

____

Keep these 4 steps in mind as you continue reading this book and stay committed to the actions that will support your own personal intention. Only you can make your dreams a reality!

In addition to your big overall intention, set an intention each morning as you awake. This could be to have a joyful and productive day.

Remind yourself of your intention throughout the day, especially if you feel stressed, if you experience negative thoughts or emotions or if you feel overwhelmed. The simple intention of having a joyful and productive day, or whichever positive intention you choose, has the power to cast away negativity and bring you back to joy and productivity.

Remember to set an intention every morning, as you continue your life's journey and the practices suggested in this book.

Don't become attached to it throughout the day, but have the intention to be in joy, to feel peace while being productive. Then if you feel stressed at any point, remind yourself of the intention to return to the beauty of the present moment. We truly can feel good and be happy most of the time, no matter what kind of work we do, what is happening with loved ones, what our financial situation is etc.

To be able to live your intention it is important to feel grounded. The following practice will help you to ground and stay focused, rather than getting distracted and pulled into other people's energies and journeys.

Grounding Practice

Stand with both feet facing forward, slightly bend your knees, shoulders rolled back, heart open. Feel that you are rooted into the earth. You can imagine roots going from the soles of your feet into the center of Mother Earth. Nothing can shake your strong foundation physically or emotionally. The earth will support you.

**I am heavenly grounded!
Deeply rooted into the earth,
I reach for the heavens
and open to all possibilities
that are in my highest and best
interest.**

I Just Want to be Happy…

What is it that you really want? A house, car, more money? What is it about that physical manifestation that you really want? For most people it is a feeling. A house makes you feel safe or successful. More money can help people feel secure. What if you focused on happiness itself? Maybe you do not even need the big house, the fast car, a million dollars to be happy. What if you could feel fulfillment in YOURSELF?

If your happiness depends on external, material items, it may not last, since no material thing lasts forever. It can be like a roller coaster, you work hard to make more money, buy what you want (do you really need it and will it make you happy in the long run?), enjoy it for a while, either until you get tired of it and you want the next thing or until it breaks down and you are off to the next thing.

Don't get me wrong, it is nice to enjoy things, there is nothing wrong with it, but if we get so attached to the material that "it" makes us happy when we have it and disappointed when we lose it or when it breaks, it is very draining. The emotional highs and lows take a lot of energy and leave us un-centered and unsatisfied.

When we let go of the attachment to material things and external experiences and focus on our internal happiness, we can achieve centeredness, balance, true happiness and peace. How can we cultivate this inner happiness and peace? Yoga and meditation are wonderful tools to find, feel, deepen and maintain physical, emotional, mental and spiritual balance, peace and happiness, the kind of peace and happiness that will last.

***"I relax and cast aside
all mental burdens,
allowing God
to express through me
His perfect love,
peace, and wisdom."***

Paramhansa Yoganandada

The Second Key - Spirituality

"Be afraid of nothing.
Hating none, giving love to all,
feeling the love of God,
seeing His presence in everyone,
and having but one desire –
for His constant presence
in the temple of your consciousness –
that is the way to live in this world."

Paramhansa Yogananda

Sustainable Happiness

Do you feel hungry for adventure, excitement, or other external stimulation?

What your heart and soul is really telling you is that deep within you are hungry for God. Nothing and no one external can truly make you happy in the long run. The only lasting happiness lies in our connection with God, the Creator. Sure, our loved ones can bring joy into our lives, but really, they can only enhance the joy that is already present within us.

God encompasses everything. When we have God in our heart and life, we have it all.

"Seek ye first the kingdom of God, and his righteousness, and all these things shall be added to you."

(Matthew 6.33)

The only sustainable happiness lies in your connection with God. Don't squirm, it is not a punishing God, it is a loving and kind God. A God of your own understanding that has your best interest at heart; a God that is supporting you, not telling you that you are wrong, guilty or bad. If you prefer a different term, simply replace it with "higher power, Creator, spirit, source, universe" or whatever resonates with you that is uplifting and supporting.

Take a moment and reflect on God. Are you comfortable with God or do you feel threatened, angry, sad, like a sinner, when you feel the energy of God by saying "God" out loud.

Who or what is God to you? A person - loving or punishing - a thought, feeling, energy, higher power, source, Creator, the universe, the divine, a force that guides you? We are constantly guided, never alone.

It is important to clearly understand how you see God and what relationship you have with God. Take a moment to reflect on your definition of God of your own understanding.

My Current Understanding of God (Journal it here)

If you feel any restrictive energy with your definition of God, replace the term with one that resonates with you, or keep the term God and create a new definition, perspective and understanding of God and your relationship with God..

God is loving and kind, supportive, and God has your best interest at heart. God guides you along your path. It is very freeing to feel at peace with God. When you no longer have resentment towards God and no longer try to push God away, God can and will actually help you.

All you need to do is to allow it, trust you deserve to feel one with God and you are worthy of feeling God's love and support.

I invite you to repeat the affirmations below.

Here's a brief guide for successful affirmations:

- With your eyes closed, gently lift your gaze to your third eye, your intuitive center between your eyebrows. This helps to connect to Truth.
- Say your affirmation out loud a few times with concentration.
- Soften your voice and repeat your affirmation several times with compassion.
- Now say it mentally (silently).

Affirmations:

- ❖ "I am worthy of God's love and support."
- ❖ "I allow God's help in my life."
- ❖ "I know that I am one with God."
- ❖ "God is loving and kind."
- ❖ "I am loved, supported and nurtured."

When you have come to terms with the term God, or whichever one you have chosen, it is a pleasure to connect with him/her/it.

When you do, you will be able to have conversations with God over time and with practice, and you will find that your prayers are answered, sometimes in meditation where you may hear the silent voice of God, sometimes throughout your daily activities. This is where awareness in the present moment becomes extremely important.

If you race through the day without consciously experiencing the Now, there is a pretty good chance that you will miss the many answers that God gives you. The more you focus on your connection with God, the more sustainable your happiness becomes. Remember, you co-create with God, God is your ally. God is pure love, pure joy, pure happiness and bliss. Why not align ourselves with the essence of these beautiful feelings?

People and things come and go, God is always present, within you and around you. God is the energy of bliss within you. Once you feel bliss within you, you are able to feel it in the external world. Meditation is the way to open up to feeling this bliss inside.

God is in every being, in plants, the ocean, animals, people, everyone and everything. It is the amazing energy of creation, the vibration that makes everything function. The more you align yourself with this unconditional love, the more stable, happy and healthy you will be.
God is prana, the life force, that flows through your whole being and through life. With an open mind and heart reflect on your new understanding of God.

My New, Positive Understanding of God:

____

____

____

____

____

____

____

____

____

____

____

____

You may wonder why this is part of the meditation chapter. You could just observe your breath and calm your mind. For a deeper experience it is so helpful to be at peace with God and allow yourself to relax into the oneness with God. To want to do that, it is important that your understanding of God is positive.

Whatever God means to you now, it is right for you. Your feelings are your reality. If something feels uplifting, it is in alignment with your truth, your essence and your higher self. Trust it for what it is at this time. It may change over time. For now it is perfect the way it is.

When we are living in alignment with not only our mind and body, but also our spirit and soul, we are living in union or "yoga". It is then that we can fully experience oneness within our whole being and with others. We are one. From this place of union and oneness, we can feel oneness with God. We are not separate. Our mind may think that we are and try to create separation. At the core we are one with God, Creator, our higher power. It is very important to reach a place of acceptance and belief in a God of your understanding. Meditation is an amazing tool to connect with God and feel that soothing, healing oneness with God.

Given that we are all one, we are God consciousness. This is not to be seen in an arrogant way as in "I am God, so I am in charge", but rather in a humble way. We are all part of God, so you are just as important as everyone else. A successful businessperson is not more important in the Creator's eyes than a homeless person. We are all children of God, divine and pure in our nature.

Religion has often been misinterpreted, misunderstood, but **the true essence of all religions is universal love**.

People who are committed to their spiritual progress and self realization sometimes choose a Guru. We can progress to a certain point by ourselves. The last steps towards liberation are often guided by a Guru who is omnipresent and knows everything we need. A Guru leads us from darkness to light, from death to immortality, to ultimate liberation. We may have several teachers, but only one Guru.

A Guru is ***"the source and inspirer of the knowledge of the Self, the essence of reality for one who seeks".***

(Vedas, hymn 4.5.6 of Rigveda)

When the student is ready the teacher will show up. We will feel in our heart when it is time for a guru to come into our lives. We will feel a deep connection, love from and for this divine being, whether he or she is in the body or no longer in physical form. There will be a deep knowing that this is the master that can and will guide us to the ultimate self realization.

The Role of Religion

***"The true basis of religion
is not belief,
but intuitive experience.
Your religion is not
the garb you wear outwardly,
but the garment of light
you weave around your heart."***

Paramhansa Yogananda

The opening of the heart must be understood as an opening of our true nature. It is not something we acquire or impose on our nature. It is something we uncover through our individual spiritual growth. It IS our true nature.

Why is it our nature? God holds this universe together by the power of love, and everything is a part of that love. Every cell of our bodies are held together through love. We are each held to one another, to life, to everything by the adhesive power of God's love.

The more we develop spiritually, the more we uncover within ourselves the heart's natural love. Swami Sri Yukteswar said, ***"The first and most essential thing on the spiritual path is to uncover the natural love of the heart; without that one cannot take one step on the spiritual path."***

Many people's spiritual practice includes worship. Devotion to God, in any of His Infinite Forms, is a critical aspect of any Spiritual Path. Deities, or physical forms of the Divine Creator (God), represent aspects of ourselves that can be helpful to develop on a deeper level. They provide us an outer physical expression from which we can tune our deeper inner Self.

Depending on your religion or spiritual attunement, you may be familiar with and drawn to a specific deity. In Hinduism, for example, Brahma, Vishnu and Shiva are considered the cosmic functions that create, sustain and destroy the universe. Christian tradition speaks of the Father, Son, and Holy Ghost.

People realized nature operates in three ways: **creative, preservative, and dissolutive**. One who attains the ultimate wisdom realizes that everything is spirit in pure essence, though hidden in manifestation. Seekers first found God by closing their eyes to shut out immediate contact with the world and matter, so they could concentrate on discovering the intelligence behind it. When they shut off the five senses, doing away with consciousness of matter, the inner world of spirit began to open up.

Whatever your religious inclination, you can realize all three aspects of the Divine operating in your life - in a simplified way they help us to start a project, persevere, and when it is time to free ourselves, transform what is no longer needed to create space for new creations. They aid in moving us along in life, through the many facets it presents, from birth to death.

Depending on what aspect in you and your life you would like to empower and energize, you can call upon any deity of any religion. For some people it is helpful to look at a physical representation to make God and divine qualities more tangible. Ultimately, it is all energy, and we are one with all that is.

Some of the world's religions (represented as only a small example of the diverse expressions of God this world embraces):

Religion	Founder	Guiding Light
Christianity	Jesus Christ	*"Blessed are the pure of heart, for they shall see God."*
Judaism	Abraham	*"Be still and know that I am God".*
Hinduism	Krishna	*"To one who is without peace, how is happiness possible?"*
Buddhism	Buddha	*"The way is not in the sky. The way is in the heart."*
Muslim	Muhammad	*"And every single favor in creation comes from Allah (God)."*
Taoism	Lao Tzu	*"To the mind that is still, the whole Universe surrenders."*
Sikh	Gurū Nānak:	*"Dwell in peace, in the home of your own Being."*
Bahai	Bahá'u'lláh	*"Be patient under all conditions, placing your trust in God."*
Zoroastrianism	Ahura Mazda	*"A reflected, contented mind, is the best possession."*

"For the Masters all come to earth for the purpose of holding up to every man a reflection of his deeper, eternal Self."

Paramhansa Yogananda

If it resonates with you, you may like to note what religion or deity you are drawn to at this time, and/or what aspect that you feel guided to cultivate at this time.

You can **pray to this deity** and thank her/him for their support.

___

___

___

There is plenty of spiritual music available online that calls upon a specific deity. Listening to these inspiring songs or chants and chanting along will help to invoke their presence and support. Call and response chanting is called kirtan[1]. Amazing kirtan artists you may like to explore are Girish, Snatam Kaur, Deva Premal, Krishna Das, David Newman, Wah, Jaya Lakshmi, and Ananda Das, just to name a few. There are also wonderful Christian musicians such as those found within the numerous music streaming services available today (search "Christian" genre).

There are many things in life that are beyond our control. We do, however, have the possibility to be responsible for our own states of mind and to change them so we can have a positive outlook on events, feelings and experiences.

Paramhansa Yogananda says, ***"Circumstances are neutral; they appear positive or negative according to the corresponding reactions of our heart."***.

We have a choice in every moment. When our mind is busy, we tend to react from emotions, not from a calm, clear space. Whether that reaction comes out in words or actions, it can be harmful to ourselves and others. Once our mind is balanced and clear, we can speak and act calmly from Truth.

Energy and Magnetism

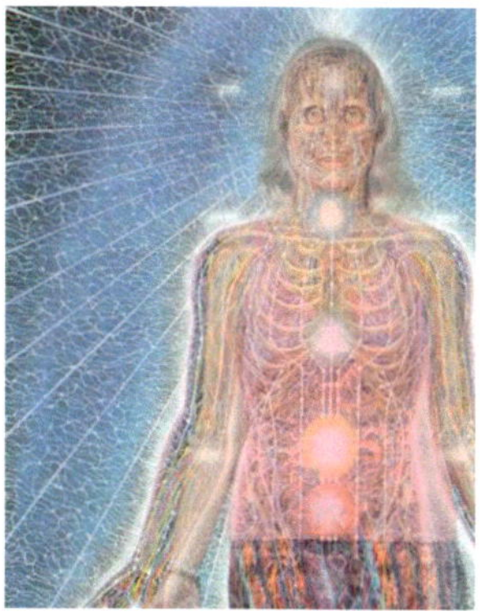

"If you want to find the secrets of the universe, think in terms of energy, frequency and vibration."

Nikola Tesla

Let's begin with a brief understanding of what energy is, its relationship to our lives, our minds, our bodies, and most importantly, our happiness. And how all Yogic Practices are meant to align us with our energy bodies.

Chakras - Your Energy Body

The chakras are the body's invisible energy centers that store information and distribute life force. When out of balance, they hold the root cause of a variety of physical illnesses, emotional disturbances, and general unhappiness with life.

CHAKRA (Location)	**COLOR**	**CHARACTERISTICS**
7th – Crown (Sahasrara)	**Violet**	**Spirituality**
6th - Third Eye (Ajna)	**Indigo**	**Awareness**
5th – Throat (Visuddha)	**Blue**	**Communication**
4th – Heart (Anahata)	**Green**	**Love, Healing**
3rd – Solar Plexus (Manipura)	**Yellow**	**Wisdom, Power**
2nd – Sacral (Svadhistana)	**Orange**	**Change, Sexuality, Creativity**
1st – Root (Coccyx) (Muladhara)	**Red**	**Basic Trust, Groundedness**

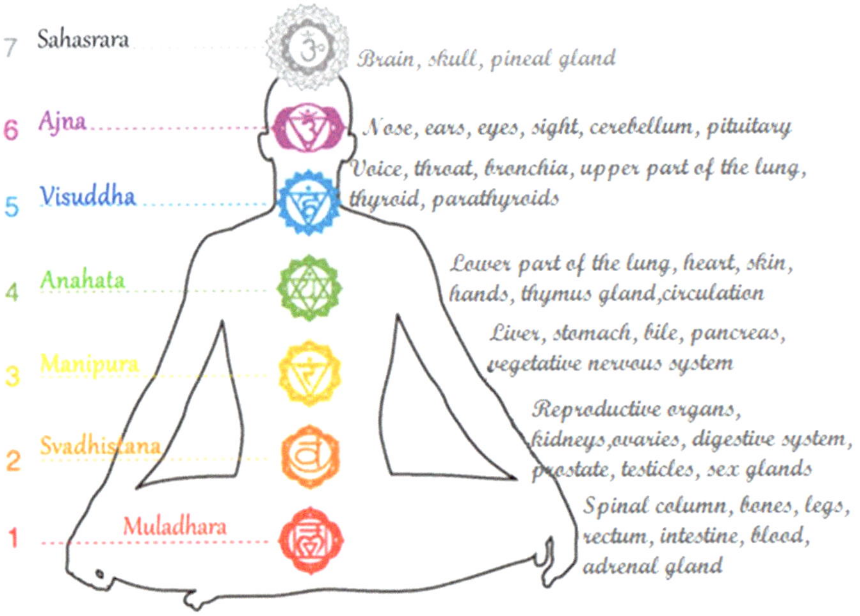

You Are MORE than the Material Body

Understanding and awakening the chakras will help you achieve a state of well-being on every level.

Once these chakras are open and balanced, the energy can flow freely through your spine and your whole being, and you can be physically and emotionally balanced and healthy. You will find specific yoga for chakra balancing in the back of this book. You can also choose to focus on or wear clothing of the color of the chakra that you like to balance.

In many yoga classes "OM" (or "AUM") is chanted. OM/AUM is the basic sound of the universe. Chanting OM tunes us into that sound and acknowledges our connection to everything in the world and the universe. The vibration has a calming effect on the body and the nervous system. Joy will arise through the depth of OM.

The light in the heart is always there. Cultivate it, and you will see and feel the light in the external reality. "Bad" feelings will change after a short time of chanting OM and practicing yoga.

Meditation as Art and Science

Meditation is a fascinating practice and a powerful tool that combines both art and science. Here's why:

The Art of Meditation:

- Mindfulness and Creativity: Think of meditation as an artistic expression within your mind. It's like painting on the canvas of your thoughts and emotions. When you meditate, you nurture qualities like mindfulness, compassion, and calmness. These are your creative brushstrokes, shaping your inner world.

- Personal Exploration: Just as artists explore their creativity, meditation allows you to explore your inner landscape. You find your own unique style and approach—one that resonates with you. Afterall, every body is different! It's about discovering what feels right and meaningful for YOU.

The Science of Meditation:

- Research and Brain Effects: Scientists study meditation to understand its impact on our brains and bodies. Through research, we've learned that meditation can actually change how our brains function. It's like unlocking hidden potential. For instance, it reduces stress, sharpens our thinking, and enhances emotional management.

- Evidence-Based Benefits: Imagine scientists peeling back the layers of our minds and bodies. They've found evidence that meditation improves our health and well-being. It's not just a feel-good practice; it's backed by data.

Spiritual Benefits of Meditation

From a spiritual perspective, meditation is about experiencing the interconnectedness of all things and understanding that we are all part of a larger, universal energy field, a universal consciousness. By working with this energy consciously and intentionally, we can tap into our inner power and potential, cultivate greater awareness and understanding, and live more fulfilling, happy, and meaningful lives.

Medical Benefits of Meditation

Research on meditation has shown that regular practice can lead to changes in the brain that are associated with improved emotional regulation, attention, and memory.

Additionally, numerous studies have demonstrated that meditation can be effective in reducing symptoms of anxiety and depression and may even enhance immune function.

Meditation has been shown to have numerous medical benefits, including:

- **Stress Reduction:** Meditation can help reduce stress and anxiety by promoting a state of relaxation and calmness. It helps to reduce the levels of cortisol (stress hormone) in the body, which can lead to improved physical, mental, emotional, and spiritual health.
- **Lower Blood Pressure:** Regular practice of meditation has been linked to lower blood pressure levels. High blood pressure is a risk factor for various health conditions such as heart disease, stroke, and kidney disease.
- **Improved Sleep:** Meditation can improve the quality and duration of sleep, leading to better physical and mental health. It has been found to reduce insomnia and improve sleep in people with sleep disorders.
- **Pain Management:** Meditation can help alleviate chronic pain by changing the way the brain processes pain signals. It has been found to be effective in reducing pain associated with conditions such as fibromyalgia, arthritis, and migraines.
- **Improved Immune System Function:** Meditation has been shown to boost the immune system by increasing the production of antibodies and activating natural killer cells, which are responsible for fighting infections and cancer cells.
- **Improved Emotional Well-being:** Meditation can help improve emotional well-being by reducing symptoms of depression and anxiety. It can also increase feelings of happiness, empathy, and compassion.

- **Improved Cognitive Function:** Meditation has been shown to improve cognitive function, including attention, memory, and executive function. It has also been found to increase gray matter in certain areas of the brain, which is associated with better cognitive function.

Overall, the medical benefits of meditation are numerous and can lead to improved physical, mental, emotional, and spiritual health.

Summary

If you're interested in incorporating meditation into your routine, try a few different styles and consider guided exercises to get started with one that suits you. The bottom line...

Meditation is something everyone can do to improve their physical, mental, emotional, and spiritual health.

JOURNAL

Building You Meditation Practice

You can do it anywhere, without special equipment or memberships.

Alternatively, meditation courses and support groups are widely available.

There's a great variety of styles too, each with different strengths and benefits. Remember, meditation is an art best practiced through techniques that align with YOUR body, mind, and spirit.

Trying out a style of meditation suited to your goals is a great way to improve your quality of life, even if you only have a few minutes to do it each day.

Meditation is a means of stilling the mind by focusing and concentrating on any single aspect of God. Peace, calmness, joy, love, wisdom are all aspects which are our birthright to embrace and to live with.

An art and a science, Meditation is for everyone, young and old. As art - everyone is unique, every practice is meant to be personalized… make it your own.

Science - thousands of years, practiced by saints and sages of all religions, it is proven effective. Recent research on meditation has shown that regular practice can lead to changes in the brain that are associated with improved emotional regulation, attention, and memory. Additionally, studies have demonstrated that meditation can be effective in reducing symptoms of anxiety and depression and may even enhance immune function.

Composed of 2 parts: Getting there (the techniques) and Being there (the connection to your own Divine Nature).

Techniques

I suggest creating a sacred space for your meditations. You can choose a picture of a saint or ascended master, light a candle, and infuse it with love or peace, burn incense with the intention to clear the space, and whatever else feels uplifting and inspiring to you.

Meditation Asanas

Pillow / Meditation Cushion | **Meditation Bench** | **Chair**

There are several aspects that will enhance your meditation practice.

First, find a comfortable seat. You may have seen lots of meditation images of people sitting cross legged. This is not a must and would not be comfortable if your knees or hips feel tight.

Depending on what feels comfortable for your body, you can sit cross legged on a pillow or meditation cushion, sit on a meditation bench or a chair (see pictures).

A meditation cushion can help to slightly tilt your hips forward, which will make it easier to sit with a straight spine.

The angle of your knees and hips on a meditation bench allows you to feel no pressure in the knees or on your feet and straighten your spine naturally.

If you choose to sit on a chair, sit away from the back, so your spine is free.

Whatever seat you choose, ideally your spine will be straight, yet relaxed, shoulders rolled back and heart open to receive. When the spine is straight, your chakras will be open, and the energy will flow freely through your spine and whole being.

For all meditations close your eyes with your gaze gently lifted to your third eye to connect with your inner wisdom and the Christ consciousness. Rest your hands on your thighs close to your abdomen with palms facing up to receive.

To deepen your connection with God at this time, and feel peaceful oneness with all that is, let's explore some meditations. Bring your awareness to your breath.

- Breathe through your nose.
- Observe your breath without changing it.
  - Where does the breath enter?
  - Where does it leave?
- Begin breathing into your belly, pushing your belly out.
- Pause at the top of your inhalation.
- Exhale, pulling your belly in towards your spine.
- Pause at the end of the exhalation.
- Continue this deep belly breathing for 24 counts or for as long as you need to feel centered and calm.
- If you are still feeling restless or anxious or are just starting to calm your mind, continue the above life force exercise with slow, calm breaths through your nose.
- Relax into this higher state of brain-wave (referred to as the Theta Brainwave)
- If thoughts distract you, don't give them any attention, rather simply return to your breath.

When you feel deeply relaxed after the above pranayama you have slowed your brain waves to 4-7 cycles per second and are in the deeply meditative theta brainwave. Be patient, and you will reach a deeper state of relaxation and meditation. Don't force it, simply allow it to happen.

This takes practice - take some time for conscious breathing every day. It will enhance everything in your life!

Below are meditations that will help you to start your day in a peaceful way, get centered if you feel stressed throughout the day, and end the day in a calm and balanced way.

For guided audio meditations I suggest my Heart Healing Meditations as well as Chakra Meditations for Humans and Animals CDs, which are available as download online.

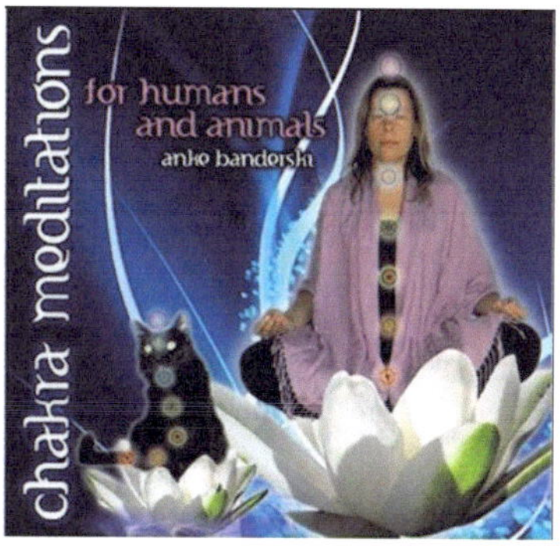

WEBSITE: https://caseyandanke.net/meditation/

For each meditation you could set a timer for one minute in the beginning, then 5 or 10, 20 or 30 minutes. The length of time is less important than the depth of your meditation.

If you are new to meditation your mind may be active, and a few seconds of focused meditation with no thoughts may be what you will experience.

Over time fewer thoughts will arise and you will feel deeper stillness, calm and peace. Even if you experience a meditation that you may judge as unsuccessful because your mind was busy, you still earn wonderful benefits.

Just like yoga, meditation is a practice. Do not get frustrated when thoughts come in, just watch them leave without judgment.

There are many wonderful tools (mobile apps) that help you enter into deeper states of meditation with guidance. Among my favorites are:

- Ananda Meditation App: https://www.ananda.org/meditation/app/
- Self Realization Fellowship App: https://yogananda.org/app-faq

"There is a light that shines
beyond the world,
beyond everything.
Beyond all,
beyond the highest heaven.
This is the light that shines
within your heart."

Upanishads

Morning Meditation

Start your day in gratitude. In the morning, as soon as you awake, begin the following practice:

- Breathe in "I am grateful and happy", breathe out anything that worries you or prevents you from feeling grateful and happy.
- Repeat this at least ten times or for as long as you need to feel grateful and happy.
- Practice the three-part yogic breath (Reduces stress and anxiety levels, improves focus and attention, cognitive performance, and improves respiratory function and cardiovascular health):
    - Breathe in through your nose, pushing your belly out. draw the same breath into your rib cage and into your chest for a total count of five or six.
    - Hold the breath for the same count.
    - Breathe out through the nose for the same count- chest, ribs, belly, and draw the belly in towards your spine.
    - Repeat this pranayama at least ten times.
- When you feel centered, return to your regular, natural breath, and notice if it has changed. It will probably be calmer and deeper. Don't judge it, just observe.

  Meditate in silence. Your gaze is gently lifted to your third eye, your spiritual center between your eyebrows.
- In this peaceful, present state you can ask the Creator what you are meant to focus on today. Listen to the answer which may come in many ways.
- At the end of your meditation, chant three Oms.

This practice sets the tone for your day, which will make it easier to stay peaceful, grateful and happy throughout the day.

Affirmation/Mantra Meditation

- Choose an affirmation to help your mind to focus, such as "I am peace" (I am saying "I am peace", not "I am at peace", given that our soul is peace), "I am calm" or "I am one with God".

- With your eyes closed, gently lift your gaze to your third eye, your intuitive center between your eyebrows. This helps to connect to Truth.
- Say your affirmation out loud a few times.
- Soften your voice and repeat your affirmation several times.
- Now say it mentally.
- When your mind is calmer, breathe slowly through your nose, and observe your breath. Your gaze is still lifted to your third eye.
- Observe your breath, and pay less and less attention to thoughts. If any thoughts enter your mind, be in acceptance of them without identifying with them, and return to your breath. Your breath is all that matters.
- At the end of your meditation, chant three Oms.

Take the peace you cultivated into the remainder of your day.

Evening Meditation

At the end of the day it is very helpful to integrate the positive experiences of the day, release limiting emotions, and feel calm energy that will allow you to sleep and rest deeply and peacefully.

- Take a few deep breaths through the nose to center yourself.
- Reflect on positive experiences you enjoyed today.
- Sigh out limiting energies from today. Let them go, even if you do not know what exactly they are. Nothing to hold onto that no longer serves you. This may take five, ten or thirty deep breaths. Continue until you feel clear and free, spacious and light.
- Breathe in gratitude, breathe out anything else you are still processing from this day.
- Breathe in peace, breathe out peace.
- Enjoy several minutes in stillness. If thoughts come in, return to observing your breath or choose an affirmation, such as "I am grateful.".
- At the end of your meditation, chant three OMs.

Allow this positive energy of gratitude and peace to guide you into deep, restful sleep.

There are many different styles of meditation, each with their own techniques. Yet all focus on the same singular purpose - to concentrate deeply on any singular quality of God, that Divine Nature within you.

Find one that resonates with you. Joining a meditation group can be helpful. A guided meditation may be easier for you in the beginning. I encourage you to also practice meditation in silence. In deep stillness is where you will find calmness, peace, joy, love.... the qualities of God that I have referred to previously.

Consistency is key for meditation, as it is for all yoga practices (i.e. postures/asanas, pranayamas, mudras, and affirmations). That's why they are called asana practice and meditation practice. Commit to meditating in the morning and in the evening. Starting the day with meditation is a wonderful way to set a peaceful tone and an unshakable foundation for the experiences of the day. Ending the day with meditation helps us to integrate positive experiences and let go of busy-ness from the day. It will help you to sleep peacefully, as you will not need to use your sleep to process the experiences of the day.

Through deep meditation you will be able to feel deep INNER peace, this kind of peace that is independent from and unrelated to external circumstances. When you meditate regularly, at least once a day, ideally every morning and evening, you will be able to maintain your inner peace more easily.

If you are uncomfortable with silence or find it harder to still your mind in silence, there are many guided meditations available. My guided meditation CD's "Heart Healing Meditations" and "Chakra Meditations for Humans and Animals" may be helpful tools for you. They are available as downloads online. Many other tools exist (see page 42) to help you build a personal meditation practice and, more importantly, begin to harvest the vast rewards it offers (sustainable happiness and peace).

It is more important to meditate for a few minutes every morning and every night than to set aside half an hour or an hour if you are just beginning to meditate. It will be challenging to focus for this length of time, and you would just be spending most of this precious time thinking rather than truly meditating. Start small and commit to a daily practice!

Do not get overwhelmed with the suggested practices. Find a way to enjoy each of the practices. **Make them your own practice.** Remember, they are all fun tools to guide you to feel good and be happy!

What does 'living a spiritual life' mean to you? Meditation? Honoring your family and neighbor? Going to church? Being of service to others?

Express in your own words how you can live a spiritual life.

____

____

____

____

____

____

____

____

____

____

____

____

I invite you to revisit what you wrote in 4 months to see what has changed.

Keep in mind that the simplest task can be done with awareness and presence in the moment, so washing the dishes, doing laundry, taking the kids to school etc. can be part of your spiritual practice. We will deepen this idea in the Purpose chapter.

"Do not condemn who you were yesterday.
Glorify who you are today,
and dream of who you can become tomorrow."

Donald Walsh

The Third Key - Yoga

"Focus your attention within.
You will feel a new power,
a new strength,
a new peace -
in body, mind and spirit.
When you do this,
all bonds that limit you
will be broken."

Paramhansa Yogananda

We are the soul, Pure Spirit, encased in a body.

The physical body in this life is our temple that houses the soul. It is not only important to nurture and respect our body so that we can experience physical health but just as important to nurture our soul. When we do not feel healthy physically, it can be challenging to focus on our soul and feel peace.

If you want to feel good, be happy and healthy, yoga is a wonderful way of life. In its truest form, yoga is a complete system for living a balanced and happy life - through right thinking, right posture, right breath, and through concentration. Since many people think yoga is a workout that only flexible people can accomplish, let me briefly explain the original meaning of yoga.

Yoga means union* and does not have to be a power workout. In fact, it does not even have to include movement of the physical body at all. A yoga practice is meant to create union with your body, mind and soul which can be achieved through "pranayama" or regulation of the breath, through movement and stillness. The true purpose of yoga is described by Patanjali in the Yoga Sutras: ***"Yoga chitta vritti nirodha."***, meaning ***"Yoga stills the fluctuations of the mind"***. Once the mind is calm, we can sit still in meditation and experience deep peace.

The past is history, the future is a mystery, and the present is a gift. Be grateful for your insights and your awareness. From now on, be present in the moment and feel out whether a choice, a conversation, a situation is uplifting or draining. Remember that you have a choice in every moment.

Affirm to yourself…

“I make conscious choices that are uplifting and support my peace, joy, balance, health and happiness.”

How do we do that?

By living a yogic life - one that integrates breath, right thinking, proper diet, asanas (yoga postures), and deep concentration (meditation) - all tools which serve to unite us to our Divine Nature.

We are often so busy thinking about the past, the future, other people, that we lose ourselves in the density of these thoughts. To come back to who we truly are, we need to let go of this restlessness, the many thoughts that are overwhelming the mind as well as the restlessness in the body.

In addition to calming the mind, yoga helps us to release restlessness from the body, which makes it easier to be present in the now. When we live in acceptance in the now, we can feel good and be happy. We are no longer pulled into past experiences or fear or worry about the future. In this moment, as you read and focus on this, everything is perfect.

Given that many of us experience restlessness in our minds as well as our physical bodies, practicing asanas can be of tremendous value. A regular practice of simple living, high thinking, right postures, conscious breath, and inner concentration will increase flexibility, health, and strength of your body. It will also balance your emotions, calm your mind and allow for a sense of oneness within your whole being and the outside world.

How can you still a mind that is constantly active? As you begin to follow through with the first three "Encapsulated Keys"- intention setting, spirituality, and yoga - you will notice that your mind becomes calmer, ever more so, at the end of those practices. Negative thoughts are not popping up as often as before, and when they do, you are able to replace them with positive thoughts. In this positive, uplifting energy, it is much easier to still the mind.

My own yoga experience has been very powerful. I felt intense knee pain for five years, even when I did not have any weight on my leg. It was diagnosed as torn cartilage. I had the surgery, and the pain persisted, even for months after physical therapy. The doctor said at that point that it was arthritis, and I would just need to live with it. One day someone asked me "Have you tried yoga?" I hadn't and thought "what is yoga going to do? Just stretching? How is that supposed to help me ?" I was desperate enough to try it and started taking yoga classes at the gym in New York that I was working out at during that time. I still remember what the yoga teacher said in my first class, even though it was 24 years ago ***"Your body is your temple."*** I had never heard that before and thought "that is so cool!" After practicing yoga twice a week for two months, my knee pain was gone! The integration of intention, affirmations, breath, movement, and meditation has not just healed my body, but allowed me to feel peace and oneness that I had never experienced previously. Yoga has been a way of life for me since then, and the pain has never come back.

So, I am telling you from direct experience that yoga works! Yoga is deeply healing for the body, mind, spirit and soul. My yoga practice helped me realize that **everything is energy**. Everything around us, inside of us, everything! If everything is energy, everything can change. Nothing is rigid, so our physical, emotional, mental and spiritual state of being can and does change. Here are a few questions to ask yourself.

Body Awareness Exercise

Do you feel aware of, and in tune with, your body?

____

____

Can you feel your body from the inside?

____

____

When you touch your skin, does it feel like it's you?

____

____

Does the lower and upper part of your body feel connected and a part of you?

____

____

How about the right and left side? Do they differ, if so, how?

____

____

____

Yoga - a Complete System for Right Living

Yoga is a 5000-year-old Indian body of knowledge. It consists of a system of energy expressed in countless forms, from sound (chanting), to color, thoughts (such as affirmations), to physical postures (asanas).

The science of Yoga originated long before the first religion or belief systems were born. Derived from the Sanskrit word "Yuj", Yoga means union of the individual consciousness or soul with the Universal Consciousness. Though many think of Yoga only as a physical exercise, the science of Yoga integrates the complete essence of Right Living.

By practicing Yoga, we come to know our Oneness with the Infinite Intelligence, Divine Love. Power, and Joy which gives life to all. This is the essence of our own true Self. Our Divine Nature.

Yoga works primarily with the energy in the body, through the science of asanas and pranayama, or "life-force control". Yoga teaches how, through proper physical postures, we can attain perfect stillness in the body. And through breath-control, we can still the mind and attain higher states of awareness.

Yoga is a physical, mental, and spiritual practice that originated in India, but it is not limited to any one country or religion. It embodies unity of mind and body; thought and action; restraint and fulfillment; harmony between man and nature; a holistic approach to health and well-being.

It is not about exercise but to discover the sense of oneness within yourself, the world and nature.

Yoga will help you to feel more in tune, connected with all parts of your body. The breath helps to realize the connection of the soul, body, mind and universe.

You may say "I can't do yoga because I am not flexible." If you can breathe, you can practice yoga. Remember, it does not have to include movement of the body. If you choose a yoga class or yoga postures at home, the main focus needs to be the breath, presence in the Now and, if you choose to move the body, the movement of the spine in six directions to open the "chakras", or energy centers, along our spine.

Basic Yoga Postures for Physical and Emotional Well-Being

These yoga postures are for all ages, levels of flexibility, fitness and yoga experience. You do not need any experience. It's not about pushing yourself. Gentle movements in attunement with your breath are very balancing for the body, mind and soul. Practice all postures while breathing deeply and slowly through the nose. Allow your breath to move your body. Always listen to your body.

Never push through pain in any of the yoga postures and exercises in this book and in your life. NO PAIN, ALL GAIN! You can practice in silence or with soft, relaxing music.

You can practice just one of the practices below, depending on what you need at this time, or all of them for complete balance. I encourage you to practice all of them on a daily basis, ideally before eating or at least one hour after eating. If you are pregnant or are experiencing strong physical pain, please consult with your physician before starting any physical practices in this book.

I invite you to chant "OM" (or "AUM") 3 times before and after each yoga practice.

1. Relaxation: Forward Bend

Forward bends calm our nervous system and are very beneficial when we like to relax. A perfect time for this practice is in the evening before going to bed and any time you feel stressed.

From standing, exhale through the nose into a gentle forward bend. Your knees can be bent, especially if you experience lower back pain. Your hands may touch your legs, the earth, or you can hold onto the opposite elbow and gently sway from side to side.

Take at least 10 deep, slow breaths through the nose in this posture. This will calm your nervous system and fill your brain with fresh oxygen and prana, life force.

Then slowly roll up on the inhalation, while drawing your belly in towards your spine to protect your lower back. **Notice how relaxed you feel.**

Chair option:

Sit on a chair. Inhale while lengthening your spine. Draw the belly in towards your spine to protect your lower back as you exhale into a seated forward bend. Your hands can touch your legs, feet or earth.

Take at least 10 deep, slow breaths through the nose in this posture. Then, with your belly drawn in towards your spine, slowly roll up on the inhalation.

Notice how relaxed you feel.

2. Energization: Backbend

Back bends energize us, create strength and flexibility in our spine and in life. A wonderful time for backbends is in the morning and any time you feel tired or rigid (physically, mentally and emotionally).

From standing, inhale your arms up above your head (or place your hands on your lower back if you feel tension in your back).

Take a few breaths, lengthening your spine, then exhale through the nose into a gentle backbend. Bend your lower, middle and upper back back, keeping your neck in alignment with the spine.

Enjoy at least three deep, slow breaths through the nose in this backbend. Your neck may thank you for not over-extending it all the way back. Inhale up, exhale your palms to your heart.

Notice how energized you feel.

Chair option:

Sit on the front part of a chair with your spine away from the back. Enjoy the same practice as described above. **Notice how energized you feel.**

3. Expansion: Side Stretch

Side stretches help us to release tension from the muscles that attach to the ribs, create opening in the hips and help our lungs to get oxygenated. In life they help us to open up to new possibilities, new ways of doing and being with increased flexibility.

From standing, inhale your arms up. Focus on lengthening and extending the torso up. Keeping the extension, exhale your right arm down to the right side while extending the left arm over to the right. Draw the belly in towards the spine, take at least five deep, slow breaths through the nose. Slowly inhale both arms up to center.

Lengthen and change sides, Keeping the extension, exhale your left arm down to the left side while extending the right arm over to the left. Draw the belly in towards the spine, take at least five deep, slow breaths through the nose. Slowly inhale both arms up to center. Exhale your arms down. **Notice how open you feel.**

Chair option:

Sit on a chair, if possible, with your spine away from the back. Enjoy the same practice as described above.

Notice how open you feel.

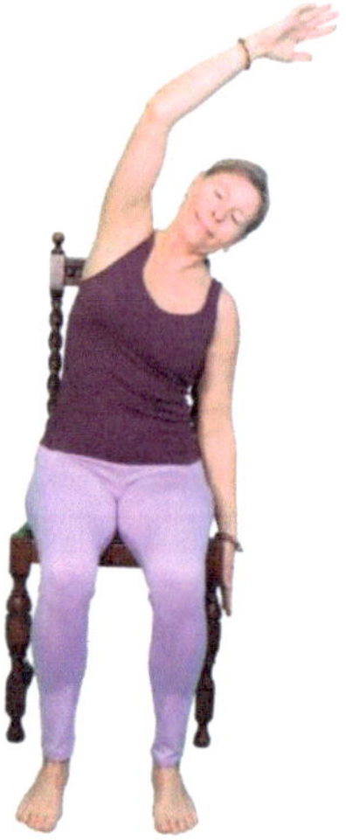

4. Release: Twist

Twists are a wonderful tool to release physical and emotional toxins, and limiting emotions, such as anger, worry, doubt, fear, anxiety, and stress.
Please do not practice twists if you are pregnant.

From seated, straighten your right leg, and flex your right foot. Bend your left leg, and place your left foot on the outside of your right leg. Lengthen your torso on the inhalation, place your right arm on the outside of your left leg and left hand behind your back on the ground with fingers pointing back. Exhale, draw your belly in towards your spine, and gently twist to the left. Take at least five deep, slow breaths through the nose. With every inhalation lengthen your torso, with every exhalation draw your belly in towards your spine and twist.

Now inhale your arms up, come to center, change legs, straighten the left leg, flex your left foot, and bend the right leg. Place your right foot on the outside of your left leg, Lengthen your torso on the inhalation, place your left arm on the outside of your right leg and right hand behind your back on the ground with fingers pointing back. Exhale, draw your belly in towards your spine, and gently twist to the right. Take at least five five deep, slow breaths through the nose. With every inhalation lengthen your torso, with every exhalation draw your belly in towards your spine and twist.

Now inhale your arms up, come to center, straighten both legs, and bring your palms together at your heart. **Notice how free you feel.**

Chair option:

Sit on a chair. Place your right knee on the outside of your left knee. Lengthen your torso on the inhalation, place your left arm on the outside of your right leg and. Your right hand can hold on to the right side of your chair back. Exhale, draw your belly in towards your spine, and gently twist to the right. Take at least five deep, slow breaths through the nose. With every inhalation lengthen your torso, with every exhalation draw your belly in towards your spine and twist.

Now inhale your arms up, come to center, change legs. Place your left knee on the outside of your right knee. Lengthen your torso on the inhalation,, place your right arm on the outside of your left leg. Your left hand can hold on to the left side of your chair back. Exhale, draw your belly in towards your spine, and gently twist to the left. Take at least five deep, slow breaths through the nose. With every inhalation, lengthen your torso, and with every exhalation, draw your belly in towards your spine and twist.

Now inhale your arms up, come to center, and bring your palms together at your heart. **Notice how free you feel.**

5. Deep Stillness: Corpse Pose

Corpse pose helps us to experience stillness in our body and mind. It is practiced after the other poses, since the previous poses help to let go of restlessness and prepare for Corpse Pose.

Lie on your back, legs slightly separated, arms alongside your body, slightly separated from your torso. Draw your shoulder blades in towards each other. Let go of any tension, and relax.

This is your opportunity for your body and mind to completely let go and just be. Observe your breath to calm your mind. A still body and mind creates deep healing. **Enjoy this pose for at least five minutes. Notice how calm you feel.**

Side-lying or chair option:

Feel free to practice this pose laying on your side or simply sit on a chair with your spine lengthened and relaxed. The essence of this pose is to relax and just be. Observe your breath to calm your mind. A still body and mind creates deep healing.

Enjoy peace during and after your practices. This present moment is our greatest gift and the only reality.

Open up and relax into feelings of peace, gratitude and joy.

JOURNAL

Now is a Great Time to Check-in

How is your intention setting, your meditation, your affirmations, and your yoga practice going? Be honest with yourself. This may be a nice time to journal about your experience of those practices. Do they feel challenging to you? Are you excited about them?

Write down how much you have been practicing each tool, and how you feel about each one.

If you are struggling with any of them, write down why that is the case.

How can you make your practice more enjoyable? It is often helpful to set specific time aside just for you, just for your own practice. Otherwise, life gets in the way. Suddenly, the day is over and you have not had a chance to practice your happiness tools.

Intention setting:

How many times per week?

____

____

Personal experience, feelings & challenges.

____

____

____

____

____

____

____

How I can and will turn challenges into joyful experiences.

Yoga practice:

This is a great time to journal about your personal experience of those practices. Do the postures feel challenging to you? Are you excited about them? Write down how much you have been practicing each, and how you feel about each one.

How many times per week

Notice how you feel after each practice. You may feel relaxed, light, free, open, flexible, and peaceful. Sometimes people say they feel tired after a practice. If you feel that, reflect on whether it is truly tiredness or actually relaxation.

Journal your insights BELOW. If you are struggling with any of them, write down why that is the case.

After your practice ask yourself the same questions that you asked before and note the difference.

Do you feel aware of and in tune with your body?

Can you feel your body from the inside?

When you touch your skin, does it feel like it's you?

Does the lower and upper part of your body feel part of you and connected?

How about the right and left side?

Personal experience, feelings & challenges.

How I can and will turn challenges into joyful experiences.

Meditation:

Number of times per day.

Personal experience, feelings & challenges.

How can you (and will you!) turn challenges into joyful experiences?

It is often helpful to set specific time aside just for you, just for your own practice. Mornings and evenings are wonderful times to practice. If you do not commit to your practice, life gets in the way, suddenly the day is over, and you have not had a chance to practice your happiness tools.

I personally have scheduled and committed time for yoga postures in my calendar. **Time for your own practice is as important as time for other people, work etc.**

Moving Forward with Your Practice

If you feel uncentered at any point during the day, just reading these reflections can motivate you to commit to an additional practice.

If you like to practice additional yoga postures in the comfort of your home, **the chapter Gentle Yoga Practices for a Balanced Life towards the end of this book is a wonderful resource.**

Also, my "Theta Yoga" CD offers a gentle Hatha Yoga practice combined with ThetaHealing that can help you to practice in the comfort of your home and eliminate the need to find a class and spend time commuting to and from a yoga studio.

My CD is available online, including on my website www.releaseintobliss.com. You can also find many yoga classes on my YouTube channel (Anke Banderski).

You may like to experience a class in person from time to time. There are many different styles of yoga and it is important to find a yoga studio, style and teacher that resonates with you. If you are new to yoga look for a gentle beginner class and always listen to and honor your body. Your body is your temple and your main teacher.

I suggest classes that focus on the spiritual aspect of Yoga, which is the true origin of Yoga, the alignment of body, mind and soul. Many classes in the Western world are workout focused, which may provide exercise but lose the essence of true yoga. Hatha, Anahata, Anusara, Kundalini, Vinyasa and restorative yoga classes are wonderful options.

Consistency

Consistency is key! Find a yoga class that you like and practice at least once or twice a week. Enjoy a practice at home every day, even if it is just for a few minutes.

Mornings are a wonderful time to practice. You will feel energized for the day, and it will help you to be focused, balanced and productive. Another great time for yoga is evenings after work to let go of the day and relax. Allow one hour after a light meal or two hours after a heavier meal before your yoga practice.

We call it "practice" for a reason. Every yoga experience builds on the next, meaning the flexibility, inner strength, focus, perseverance and peace gets stronger over time. You can practice the same postures every day and enjoy a completely new experience each time. Allow and choose a beginner's mind and ever new joy in each moment. You do not need to practice complicated postures to be a great yogi. Remember that yoga means union. The purpose of yoga is to feel union with your body, mind, spirit, soul and the Creator of all that is.

You want to feel good and be happy, right? Commit to it and, after the initial challenges of starting a new practice, you will realize that you feel happier and healthier when you practice yoga regularly.

It may even motivate you to a healthy, meaningful lifestyle including going to bed earlier, eating healthy etc. Are you wondering how long you will need to practice for? Ideally, yoga is a lifelong journey. It is an enjoyable journey of breathing, stretching and, on a deeper level, of discovering your true self and returning home to your soul.

As I already mentioned, yoga extends way beyond the yoga mat! Intrigued? Look up the "Eight Limbs of Yoga" and Patanjali's Yoga Sutras. Don't get overwhelmed, first focus on finishing this book with all its suggested practices as a foundation.

JOURNAL

"Choose happiness.
It just feels better."

Dalai Lama

The Fourth Key - Positive Affirmations & Healing

What thoughts are running through your mind most of the time?

Do you feel that you are in charge of your thoughts, or do your thoughts take over and are in charge of you? Do your thoughts weigh you down, or do they lift you up? Do you have tapes running in your mind, telling you that you are not enough, unworthy, wrong, bad, guilty or other types of judgment and self-blame, criticism and victimhood?

"Keep your thoughts positive because your thoughts become your words. Keep your words positive because your words become your behaviors. Keep your behavior positive because your behaviors become your habits. Keep your habits positive because your habits become your values. Keep your values positive because your values become your destiny."

Mahatma Gandhi

We can consciously make the choice of thinking positive, uplifting thoughts. What would you like to hear from your loved ones? Can you tell yourself these same loving words out loud and silently, mentally in thought form?

What would you like to experience and attract into your life? Joy, love, peace, balanced health, abundance, happiness, bliss, a successful career, harmonious relationships? To feel and experience this we need to let go of pain, shock and trauma, so it no longer covers up joyful feelings that are already in our hearts and souls.

If we experience challenges in life, we need to commit to feeling peace and joy inside of us. It is always there. Sometimes it is just covered up by fear, doubt, anger, and other emotions.

Once we feel peace within us, we can feel peace with other people and in our environment.

Detach from Your Story

Who are you without your story? You do not need to hold on to old pain to know who you are. Who are you without pain, trauma , drama, and the story? How would you feel if today was a new chapter in your life? A new beginning.

This moment is all we have. See it as a blank canvas. This is your opportunity to create a new reality with unconditional love, self-acceptance, self-compassion, acceptance, and compassion for the world. You will now start writing the script of the life you really want and deserve. You are able and capable to live this new supportive reality in this current incarnation, in this moment of your life.

You are divine, a spark of the universe, a child of God, just like every person in this world. You are made in the image of a loving God, so you *are* love. Your essence is pure love. Painful experiences may have distorted your self image. Deep within your soul you know that you are love. Paramhansa Yogananda shares the wisdom that "The basic You is the infinite in its potentiality." The basic you is without limiting energies.

It is time to peel off those layers of disappointment, pain, doubt, and fear. Just as we use a broom to sweep up leaves or dirt, we will use powerful tools to brush away negative, limiting thoughts and emotions, to reveal the joy and peace that is in your heart and soul.

Take a moment to center yourself through the following pranayama, life force exercise.

Brahmari Pranayama (Bee Breath)

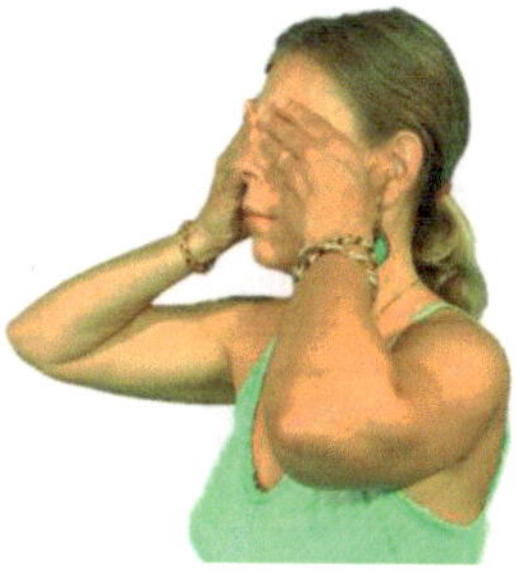

Take a few deep breaths. Place your thumbs on your ears and remaining fingers on your eyes, covering your ears and eyes to help you to go within.

Breathe in through your nose, and start humming at the pitch of your normal speaking voice. The sound is "mmmmmmm".

Gently press the rear of your tongue against the roof of your mouth. Inhale silently through the nose, hum on the exhalation. Repeat for one minute or for as long as it is comfortable. If you feel dizzy, return to your regular breath. Notice how calm and clear you feel. From this clear space you are now ready to be open and receptive to choose a positive life.

Positive Affirmations

Below are simple, uplifting affirmations as examples of how to create a positive mindset and reality.

Affirmations are positive statements that are repeated with the goal of promoting a particular mindset or belief. There is a growing body of scientific evidence suggesting that affirmations may be helpful for managing stress, anxiety, and depression, which are common co-occurring conditions with chronic pain. Modern research has shown that this practice can reduce stress, improve immune function, and enhance cardiovascular health.

In addition, studies have demonstrated that affirmations can improve mental health outcomes, such as reducing symptoms of anxiety and depression. Studies have also found that practicing affirmations was associated with significant improvements in pain intensity and pain interference, and that participants who practiced self-affirmation reported less negative effects in response to pain and an increased capacity of self-healing.

If you feel that you do not know how to live without anger, resentment, grief, self-sabotage, feelings of inadequacy, and other limiting emotions, affirm that you know how to live without those. Then also affirm that you know how to live with joy, love, gratitude, and whichever supportive feelings you need. If you feel sad or frustrated, affirm "I feel joy" or "I choose joy". Given that our soul is joy, peace and love, and we are the soul, you can take your affirmation to the next level, and affirm "I am joy."

Focus on one affirmation at a time to give it your full attention and allow the richness of each feeling to fill and nurture you.

For the strongest benefit, close your eyes, gently lift your gaze to your spiritual eye, your intuitive center, between your eyebrows, and repeat the affirmation of your choice out loud several times while feeling it in your heart.

Then soften your voice and continue repeating the same affirmation.

Eventually repeat it silently, mentally.

Enjoy a few minutes in silence to allow your mind, body, and soul to absorb and integrate the vibration of the affirmation. Be present in the moment to feel the energy of the affirmation.

You can also repeat your affirmation during activities with your eyes open. The mind likes to be busy, so let's feed it something positive to think about and focus on throughout the day.

The more present you are when you repeat your affirmation, the more you will believe it and know that it is true.

Our mind creates our reality. Choose to be happy and you will be happy. Tell yourself you are tired, and, yes, you will be tired!

Throughout this book you will find additional helpful affirmations. I encourage you to use the same process for those.

Repeat the following affirmations that will help you in an encouraging, supportive way.

Letting Go Affirmations

- "I choose to live without pain, shock, trauma, chaos, and drama."
- "I know how to live without pain, shock, trauma, chaos, and drama, and I do."
- "I know how to live without self-doubt, self-sabotage, and self-sacrifice, and I do."
- "I know how to live without neglect, rejection, and abandonment, and I do."
- "I am no longer addicted to pain."
- "I know who I am without these restrictive emotions, and I am whole and complete without them."

Feel free to add any additional affirmations that will help you to live without negative emotions. Avoid saying "not", as the subconscious mind does not always understand it. "No" and "without" is fine.

When you feel that you are complete without pain, it is much easier to allow supportive feelings to arise. Deep breathing will assist you in letting go of limiting energies.

Choosing Love, Joy, and Peace

Joy, love, and peace all start within us. We cannot expect world peace if we do not feel peace within us and with the people closest to us.

What would happen if you consciously chose to feel and be in joy? You know that you deserve it! As you wake up in the morning, commit to feeling joy.

Joy Affirmations

- "I know what joy feels like."
- "I am committed to feeling joy,"
- "I am joyful and share this joy with the world."
- "I am joy."
- "I deserve to feel joy within and around me."
- "I am worthy of joy."
- "I have the right to feel joy."
- "It is possible for me to feel joy."
- "I know what it feels like to feel joy."
- "I know how to live in joy, and I do."
- "I feel joy by myself and with others."
- "I stay joyful, even when others are struggling."
- "I trust that my joy will last."

Love Affirmations

- "I know what unconditional love feels like."
- "I am loved by the Creator."
- "I am love and share this love with the world."
- "I am lovable."
- "I believe in true love."
- "I deserve unconditional love."
- "I am worthy of unconditional love."
- "I know that love is safe and enjoyable for me."
- "I know what it feels like to give and receive unconditional love."
- "I know how to live in love, and I do."

- "I share love without depleting myself."
- "I share love without fearing that I'll lose it."
- "I trust love."
- "I trust that love will last."

Peace Affirmations

- "I know what peace feels like."
- "I am peaceful and share this peace with the world."
- "I am peace."
- "I deserve to feel peace within and around me."
- "I am worthy of peace."
- "I have the right to feel peace."
- "It is possible for me to feel peace now."
- "I know what it feels like to feel peace."
- "I know how to live in peace, and I do."
- "I feel peace by myself and with others."
- "I stay peaceful, even when others are struggling."
- "I trust that my peace will last."

Everyone wants to be happy. The difference between joy and happiness is that joy is an inner feeling, happiness an outward expression. Below are happiness affirmations, so that after you have cultivated inner joy, you can embrace happiness.

Happiness Affirmations

- "I know what it feels like to be happy."
- "I am happy."
- "I deserve to feel happy."
- "I am worthy of feeling happy."
- "I have the right to be happy."
- "It is possible for me to be happy."
- "I know what it feels like to be happy."
- "I know how to live in happiness, and I do."
- "I trust that my happiness will last."

Additional Positive Affirmations

- ❖ "I am self-confident."
- ❖ "I choose peace and harmony within me and with others."
- ❖ "I trust myself and my choices."
- ❖ "I am blessed."
- ❖ "I am loved, respected and appreciated for exactly who I am."
- ❖ "I love, respect and appreciate myself and others."

What affirmation do you need most at this time?

____

____

____

Focus on the affirmation that will serve you most. Your yoga and affirmation practice prepares you for meditation so ideally you will set time aside right after those practices to meditate.

When you practice intention setting, yoga, affirmations and meditation you are creating a spiritual way of life, of living and being. There are many ways of living a spiritual life. **Can you name a few here?**

____

____

____

____

____

____

____

____

____

____

Let's Check-in on Your Affirmation Practices:

How many times per day?

Personal experience, feelings & challenges.

How can you (and will you!) turn challenges into joyful experiences?

Changing Limiting Behaviors and Patterns

Have you ever really thought about the impact that sayings and collective consciousness beliefs create? If the same thought is released into the universe by many people, it will multiply through the law of attraction. Subconsciously we often take them in and form our beliefs.

You have a choice to hold on to those beliefs or change them to what is beneficial for you.

You may still have beliefs from your ancestors, such as "I have to work myself to the bones to earn a living".

Reflect on which beliefs you have that are from your parents, grandparents, or even further down your genetic line. **Write them down here.**

____

____

____

____

____

____

____

Which of those beliefs are beneficial and uplifting to you at this point in your life? Some of them may still serve you, some may need to be adjusted, and some may not serve you at all.

Add "B" for beneficial, "A" for adjust and "N" for not needed anymore behind your list above.

Your ancestors may have believed they needed to work hard at all times. Maybe you don't share that belief, so you can adjust it to "I have a choice as to when to work hard and when to take it easy in my highest and best way."

Choose what is energizing, empowering, and supportive for you today, and set yourself free, while honoring your ancestors. Adjust the "A"s in a way that they are beneficial for you today and from now on.

What are your adjusted, supportive beliefs?

____

____

____

____

You are no longer a victim to your genetic beliefs but empowered to consciously choose.

Affirm that you are letting go of those beliefs that no longer serve you with gratitude and respect towards your ancestors. They worked hard to have those beliefs and needed some of those beliefs to survive.

I Am Free!

You are you. You are not your parents, your ancestors, your friends, or your partner. You do not even need to live up to their expectations. You are free to be uniquely you. Everyone is given free will. You have the right and wisdom to make your own decisions, to choose your beliefs, values, and create your life in a way that is uplifting for you, with respect towards the people in your life. When you come from a place of unconditional love, you can co-create your life in a nurturing way that is not selfish. You can practice self-love and love for others. This is the way to create and maintain a spiritual practice and healthy way of life.

How can you be serious about your path and practice while staying in a space of love for yourself, others and God? Let's preserve and cultivate what is serving us and transform what is no longer beneficial.

To change the outcome of a situation, you need to change your thoughts and feelings about yourself, people involved in the situation, and the situation itself.

As Paramhansa Yogananda said, *"All circumstances are neutral."* and *"Will power turns thoughts into actions"*. **Are you willing to change?**

With the right will power, you are able to change your thoughts and feelings, and create a new outcome.

Thoughts and feelings => behaviors and patterns => outcome

(law of cause and effect)

Everything starts within us.

We need to feel joy, love, peace etc. within ourselves first before we can truly experience these beautiful feelings with and from other people. Through the law of attraction we attract the same energy that we send out into the universe. When we are happy and at peace, we naturally shine these energies out into the world. We attract more happiness and peace into our lives as well as people who vibrate in the frequencies of happiness and peace. We co-create a win, win situation!

When we live in a state of joy, love, gratitude and peace, our physical bodies heal as well.

Every physical ailment usually has an emotional connection. This does not mean that we need to avoid feeling emotions, it means that it is important to feel emotions, and let them go. What we focus on persists and increases. If you choose to focus on pain and suffering, it will increase. If you choose to focus on happiness, pain will subside, and happiness will increase.

My own traumatic experience, having had a miscarriage, made me consciously aware of the choices I faced to move forward. I could look at a beautiful palm tree which I love, and feel peace, or my mind could go into what just happened, and re-experience the shock and trauma. I was able and free to choose what to focus on in each moment, and both felt important.

Let's be real with what we feel, humanly and in the bigger picture, from our and from the Creator's perspective. From my human perspective it was a painful, disappointing, sad experience. From the Creator's perspective it was not the right time for this unborn soul to incarnate. Both perspectives were valid and real. Mine was not wrong, it was just my perspective from the pain body that I was in.

It does not serve us to stay stuck in trauma or drama. When someone has passed away, we often fear moving forward because we are afraid of disconnecting from our loved one of losing him or her completely. We try to hold on to stay close. In reality it is impossible to lose them. We are all always connected, and we continue to be able to communicate with them. As the souls that we are, we are all one.

We may be afraid that we are not perceived as compassionate if we choose to move forward peacefully, instead of continuing to suffer. When we choose peace, we can still care deeply about the person or animal that has left the body.

The more we align our truth about everything and everyone with the Creator's truth, the more joyful our whole being and life will be. In my post-miscarriage experience I did choose to look at the palm trees that make me feel uplifted more and more often, focused on that, rather than the pain, and this uplifting energy replaced the sadness. I communicated with the soul, and knew it was in a good place.

We co-create our reality, and how we feel. Through free choice, will power, and perseverance let's commit to feel good and be happy!

When we make happiness, in the now, our focus, while trusting our journey and outcome, we can extend happiness from one moment to the next, to the next, to the next... soon we can extend it from a few seconds to several minutes to a whole day.

Happiness is a choice, and so is suffering. When we are happy within us, we attract happy people and joyful situations. Feeling and expressing gratitude shifts us from pain into joy, peace, acceptance, and happiness.

Write down ten things you are grateful for. This can include a safe home, clean water, people, pets, experiences, etc..

1.____

2.____

3.____

4.____

5.____

6.____

7.____

8.____

9.____

10._______________________________________

Make this a continuous practice every night before you go to bed. This will help you to sleep peacefully, and your sleep cycle will fortify your state of gratitude.

Release Limiting Beliefs!

While affirmations are helpful, you may find that some limiting emotions and beliefs can still arise. If you like to take your transformation to a deeper level, you may like to consider the powerful energy healing technique ThetaHealing®.

ThetaHealing is a very effective tool to shift from physical and emotional pain to peace, from feeling hopeless, stuck and limited to feeling trusting, healthy and clear. It helps us to clear the root cause of painful emotions, such as anger, resentment, regret, sadness, grief, self-doubt, and fear, and replace it with supportive feelings, such as joy, gratitude, trust, unconditional love, compassion, and peace. It allows us to shift out of unhealthy patterns, behaviors and choices and create a new, positive reality.

It also allows us to release limiting subconscious beliefs that are keeping us stuck, in pain and limited, and replace them with supporting beliefs on four levels. Through this process we close neural pathways for limiting beliefs and create new neural pathways for supporting beliefs.

Vianna Stibal, the founder of ThetaHealing, healed her cancer through this technique. I am grateful for her healing, and that she shared this amazing tool with the world! In this chapter you will learn how to discern what beliefs you may have that block you physically or emotionally. You can then consciously breathe them out, so you will no longer be a victim to them.

Messages that we have received from our parents, teachers, friends and others, as well as experiences we have lived through, lead us to form beliefs - some that support us, and others that block or restrict us. We may feel that we could be healthier or happier, but we do not know what exactly is preventing us from experiencing that consistent health and happiness.

We have free will and choice in every moment. How do we perceive our world? What energies and messages do we choose to allow in?

Have you ever wondered why you take certain actions that you know are not beneficial to you? Why do you not do what you know would benefit you? Why do you procrastinate? Smoke? Drink? Not exercise? Overeat? And how can you change it? How is it serving you? What is something positive that is coming out of this destructive, self-sabotaging behavior?

Why do you feel undeserving or inadequate? Where did this come from? Who told you that? When did it start? These can be insightful questions to ask to discover the root cause or self sabotaging behaviors, and then be able to release it.

Maybe the root cause is not even from this life, but ancestral, and still carried in your DNA. Certain patterns may have served your ancestors for survival, but possibly harm you or hold you back if you continue those patterns. They may have started in a different space or time/past life and are carried over to this life and dimension in your soul.

88% of what happens inside of us is subconscious. Through the powerful energy healing technique ThetaHealing we are able to pinpoint what exactly is holding us back when we do not consciously know. We are then able to release limiting subconscious beliefs and emotions on the history, core, genetic and soul level, and replace them with positive, supporting beliefs..

History level:
Beliefs formed through our experiences and messages from past lives as well as through the collective consciousness

Core level:
Beliefs from our conception in this life until now

Genetic level:
Beliefs, patterns, and behaviors that are in our DNA from our ancestors

Soul level:
Beliefs that encompass all that we are

Where do our morals originate from? Maybe our parents' teachings, values learned from the collective consciousness, our soul and even our ancestors. Our ancestors' beliefs are still stored in our DNA, some to our benefit in this life and some not.

Your ancestor's drive to fight was needed for survival - it may still benefit us to keep this need to fight, but we have the power and right to modify how we work with it. We can have a different discernment on when to use this energy to fight for or against something and when to surrender and trust the flow.

You can reprogram your conscious, subconscious mind, and DNA, and free not just yourself, but your genetic line going back and forward in time.

When we have beliefs from our parents' teachings or past experiences, such as "I will be punished", "I have to suffer", "I am unworthy" etc., we subconsciously send the energy of those limiting beliefs out into the universe and attract people and situations that hold the same frequency. It is as if the universe was saying "Oh, you believe that you have to suffer? OK, let me bring you a relationship that is challenging and in which you experience suffering. This will allow you to hold onto it and live out your belief in the way that you are familiar with." Someone's entire life can be based on the belief "I have to suffer."

The person experiences suffering in various situations and never seems to be able to attract and live in happiness. Once we decide to let go of this limiting belief and replace it with the belief "I am happy, and I deserve to be happy, and I know how to live without suffering", the universe MUST respond in a positive, supporting way.

Suddenly we attract happy people, relationships in which we feel happy, and since we feel happy, we attract more and more happiness into our lives.

JOURNAL

Seeing the Positive in Everything

Paramhansa Yogananda states that ***"All circumstances in life are neutral. How we respond or react is our choice."*** We can find something positive in every experience. As you are reading this, you may feel stuck in a certain area of your life. Reflect on what the lessons are that you may be learning at this time. How is your experience serving you? This challenge could actually teach you something valuable.

Your first response may be "it is not!" Sometimes pain keeps us from going out into the world and being active, so it keeps us safe. When we are in pain, we can relax at home, don't need to meet new people, don't need to interact with the outside world that may seem harsh to us. As long we believe that the pain is keeping us safe, there is little motivation to let go of the pain.

What would happen if you felt safe in this world, with other people, in new situations? Then you will no longer need to hold on to the pain, and it may simply disappear. You will need to believe that you are safe with every ounce of your being. If you consciously believe it but your subconscious is doubting it, you may still not feel safe.

Many times, an accident or injury is a stop sign on our way to help us to slow down or to stop. We receive many little messages along the way, but if we are too busy to notice them, something larger is going to happen that is going to demand our attention. An injury, accident, the loss of a job or another big event is sure to get our attention. It is extremely important to stop, take a break from your regular activities and sit down. Show the universe that you are listening. You understood the stop sign and you are actually stopping.

Everything happens for a positive reason. If we experience a conflict with someone in our life, which in turn motivates us to take positive action, there is a beneficial reason for the conflict. Once we trust that we can take positive action without needing conflict in our life, the conflict will disappear. It no longer needs to teach us anything.

We co-create our life with every breath and every step along the way. Do you ever feel that you are a victim? That someone did something harmful to you? Step back and reflect on that situation. Look at the bigger picture. Could you have possibly co-created this situation, at least to a certain extent? Could you have attracted it subconsciously to learn or experience a soul quality on a deeper level?

I invite you to reflect on your life, and make a list of what you feel is blocking you, creating pain or struggle physically or emotionally. Reflect on all areas of your life.

Keep "What Can I Learn From It" open for now. We will come back to this in a moment.

Struggle (Situation, behavior, pattern...)	What Can I Learn From It?

We create our reality. In some way, you have attracted those conflicting situations into your life. This is not to blame or criticize you, it is simply to bring to your awareness that everything starts within us. We really do create our own reality through our thoughts, beliefs and experiences.

Let's go back to your struggles, so you can resolve them.

- How are they serving you?
- What good is each one doing for you?
- What are they teaching you or what could they teach you?
- What are you learning or could you learn from them in a positive way?

Close your eyes, and let the answers come to you.

Write down the first answer you receive next to "Struggle", in the table above labeled "What Can I Learn From It?" Do not analyze it; it does not need to make logical sense to you. It may keep you safe subconsciously. If you are overweight, it may subconsciously serve to keep you safe. You may feel that you do not need to go out to meet new people because of it, which could prevent you from feeling disappointed and getting hurt.

Look at each struggle and determine how it is serving you in your life. **Write it down.**

You need the awareness to know the lesson in this situation, then trust that you have learned it, it is complete, and you can move forward without needing the lesson or challenge any longer. **The struggle can now melt away,** given that it no longer needs to be our teacher or motivator. It no longer has a purpose.

Nothing and no one (external) can make us feel upset, angry, sad, frustrated, just like nothing and no one can make us feel happy, fulfilled or at peace.

These are internal feelings and emotions. If we do not feel joyful within ourselves, it is impossible for someone else to make us feel joyful. If we do not know what happiness feels like, because we have never experienced true happiness in this life or at least not in a long time, we cannot attract it since we do not know what to look for.

True happiness comes through an open heart, universal love and trust in the universe, God, the Creator, our higher power. If we feel happy in one situation and sad in the next one, we are not truly happy at the core. Happiness can be a regular state of being that is not fluctuating. It is everlasting, always present. It can be a solid foundation that remains even when we experience challenges.

It is knowing that everything is O.K. and perfect exactly the way it is. There are no mistakes, no luck, no accidents. There is a perfect divine plan for each one of us. I think we can agree on the fact that the Divine, the Creator, God is omnipresent and omnipotent with a lot more wisdom than our ego minds. So why not surrender with trust in God? Surrender does not mean giving up or giving in. It is a strength, just as acceptance is a strength. . When we surrender and accept what is, we are present with the experience without judgment. There is strength, power, and peace in this way of being and living.

Are you ready to release struggle and pain? Breathe it out, let it go.

Breathe in peace and gratitude. Set an intention NOW to align your truth about the situation with the Creator's truth. Trust that you know what to do, that which is in your highest and best interest. Focus on forgiving the people involved in you experiencing this struggle, the Creator, and yourself.

Now take action from a calm, clear space, or choose not to take action, based on the guidance you get from the Creator of All That Is.

Clear entanglement. Don't let your family run you and your life. Everyone is responsible for their own life. You may have taken on your parents' or siblings' limiting energy, which can create tension and pain in your body. Let it go. Let them be responsible for their own lives.

Heal the old you, your inner child, and integrate the old, healed you into the current you. Letting go, forgiving and loving yourself and others unconditionally is the way to go.

World peace starts with inner peace and peace with people close to us. Cultivate your inner peace rather than participating in peace marches. Do you find yourself fighting for peace or fighting for love? Do you believe that life is a fight? Let go of the energy of fight, and embrace acceptance. Then commit to peace.

Thoughts have real substance! When we are in a meditative theta brainwave, what we think can instantly manifest. Yogananda's chant "Who is in my temple" is an inspiring way of thinking and living: "All the doors do open themselves; all the lights do light themselves. Darkness like a dark bird flies away, oh flies away."

Light is stronger than darkness. Love is stronger than fear.

Let go of fear and control, and learn to trust in God, your higher power.

JOURNAL

Release Old Limiting Beliefs

Breathe out the following old beliefs that no longer serve you. Let them leave your mind and body. There is no need to hold onto anything that no longer serves you.

- "Life is a fight."
- "There is always something to fight for or fight against."
- "I have to fight for peace and love."
- "I have to fight for what I really want."
- "Life is boring without anything to fight for or against."
- "I am nothing without conflict or fight."

Replace them with New Supportive Beliefs

Breathe in the following supportive beliefs. They're similar to affirmations. Invite them into your mind and body.

- "I am in acceptance of what was, is, and will be."
- "I surrender to the Creator, and trust that it is safe."
- "I am at peace."
- "Peace and love come to me easily and effortlessly."
- "I am peace."
- "I am filled with love."
- "I live in trust and faith."
- "Truth, love, and light always prevails."

Can you think of any other old beliefs no longer serving you?

Well let's discuss a powerful tool you can use to help determine what beliefs you hold are serving you or not.

Applied Kinesiology aka Muscle Testing

Applied Kinesiology, also referred to as muscle testing, is a powerful tool that shows you through your own body if something is in your highest and best interest. Every moment is different, so it is about this moment. You need to be hydrated for this tool to work consistently.

Stand up, close your eyes, and say "yes" out loud. Without consciously moving your body, you will notice that your body will move forward.

Close your eyes and say "no" out loud. Without consciously moving your body, you will notice that your body will move back.

If it is challenging for you, it may help you to stand facing North and drink water.

You can practice this by saying "My name is *<your name>*", and "My name is *<someone else's name>*".

Now that you have established a clear yes and no, you can test a limiting belief that you think you have, and notice if your body moves forward or back. If you do not fully trust your body or the response you are receiving from your body or wonder if your mind is influencing it, add "without my mind influencing it".

You could test "I love myself no". As the subconscious mind does not understand "not", we say "no" at the end, instead of saying "I do not love myself." If you move forward, you do not love yourself.

"I am unworthy." If you move forward, you believe that you are unworthy. We could test "I love myself" and "I am worthy", but you may get a yes and also get a yes for "I love myself no" and "I am unworthy." This would be a case of a dual belief.

Exercise

What are your limiting beliefs?

Breathe each one out, and have a clear intention, knowing, and commitment to let it go completely from your mind and body.

What are you choosing to replace each belief with, so that you will not feel an emptiness without the limiting belief? What positive beliefs feel nurturing, supporting, and uplifting to you? **Journal them here:**

Breathe in each one.

Allow them to become integrated and one with your whole being.

Each person is a reflection of ourselves, mirroring our thought forms, beliefs, behaviors, and patterns. Our outer reality is a reflection of our inner state of being.

The expression often used in India is "as within, so without".

And still, everything can change, everything is possible, as long as we believe it. The more limiting beliefs and emotions we clear, and the more positive beliefs and feelings we embrace, the healthier, happier and purer we become physically, emotionally, mentally and spiritually.

Once we believe that we deserve to be happy and at peace, that it is possible for us, and we know what it feels like, we can actually start feeling these wonderful feelings more deeply, consistently, and co-create a healthy, happy and peaceful life.

There is no reason to stay stuck in any way!

ThetaHealing helps you to re-program what we just covered on the deep history, core, genetic, and soul level. It goes even deeper than breathing out the negative energy. It empowers you to live even more deeply with ease, grace, joy, gratitude, and peace!

There are many ThetaHealing recordings on my YouTube channel that you are welcome to freely enjoy (https://www.youtube.com/@ReleaseIntoBliss).

I offer private ThetaHealing sessions and certification workshops in Encinitas, California, USA, as well as Online.

Learning ThetaHealing will provide you with an extraordinary healing tool for yourself and other people, animals, plants and planets.

Visit my website
www.ReleaseIntoBliss.com
to learn more.

"Our bodies are our garden. Our wills are our gardeners."

William Shakespeare

The Fifth Key - Physical Health

"It is health that is the real wealth and not pieces of gold and silver."

Mahatma Gandhi

Physical health and well-being is important for a high quality of life. We can have abundant financial wealth, but if we do not feel healthy we will not be able to truly enjoy it. We need to be proactive in manifesting and maintaining optimum health without becoming overly attached to the physical body. Take action, infuse it with spirit, and let go with complete trust and faith in the universe's support.

My Body Hurts - What's Going on?

A physical imbalance often has an emotional or mental connection. Anger can be held in the liver, fear in the kidneys, sadness and grief in the lungs. Negative thoughts can also send limiting messages to the body. If we keep unresolved emotions or thoughts in our body and mind, it can create dis-ease in our bodies and lives over time. Breathe out the limiting energies for a healthy body and mind!

In my healing sessions, I often ask people how they feel physically, emotionally, mentally and spiritually. Everything is connected, and many times physical pain is the result of emotional struggle that, over time, got stored in the physical body and manifested as stuck energy and pain.

Once we get in touch with what happened in our lives when the physical pain started, we can pinpoint the emotional charge that is related to it. You may have back pain that started when you got divorced. At the time, you felt rejected, neglected, left alone and unsupported. These painful emotions and limiting beliefs about yourself may still be in your mind and body today.

Back pain is often related to feeling unsupported. With this awareness, you can now choose to let go of the feeling of being unsupported and focus on allowing support in, from the Creator, family, friends, co-workers. Once the painful emotion and belief is resolved, in this example, feeling unsupported, and replaced with a positive, supporting feeling, such as support, the physical pain can dissolve, and your back will heal.

What Pain are You Carrying (Needlessly)?

For me, it started with a fall; at least so I thought. I gave Jessy, my dog, a bath, then she walked through the bathroom to the bedroom, as she usually did. I walked through the bathroom and slipped on the wet floor. Yes, of course I dried her off, but she shook some additional water off her coat as she walked through the bathroom, and the floor got wet. Bam, I fell on my tailbone, and it hurt "like hell"!

For the next 5 years I have felt tension in my lower back, sacrum, hip area most of the time. Through yoga I discovered that Triangle pose helped to release tension. Through ThetaHealing commands, such as "I know how to live without pain", "I forgive Jessy, myself and the Creator for allowing it to happen" and many other releases of beliefs and emotions I have felt some nice shifts and some relief. In meditations I have been able to go beyond the body and feel no tension.

But to be perfectly honest, even after 5 years of daily work on this, including lots of gratitude for moments of being pain and tension free, I still hadn't been able to figure out the root cause, or at this point maybe the angle that I hadn't looked at yet. There it was... I intuitively received the guidance to look at other people's genetics.

I had done lots of genetic work on myself, including on this injury, but not enough with regard to the cultures of other people's genetics who were close to me.

Then the Creator told me "Look at parents' cultures of your present and past relationships." I followed through with that guidance and realized that deep in my DNA I was carrying old ancestral feelings of defeat that played out as tension in my muscles, and joints in my lower back and in my nervous system.

Our ancestors had to work hard and at times fight to survive. This created beliefs, such as "I have to fight to be safe", "I have to victimize others in order for me not to be victimized by them." etc.

You may think "OK, but this was a long time ago; we are over that." Guess what... We still carry those deep, old beliefs in our genes, unless we have worked through them and let them go. Some of them are serving us, and others no longer serve us, but they have gotten us to where we are today.

That's why, when we choose to let go of a belief, it is important to release it with gratitude.

The belief "I am defeated by a specific country" (several countries in my case) was what was still creating pain in my back. I went through my current and past boyfriend's parents' cultural backgrounds and released this belief for each country that I felt defeated by. It wasn't many different countries, but those few that came up held a strong charge.

With the release of the belief, I felt a beautiful energetic release in my back and a relief much beyond the physical plane. It felt very personal and deep. The physical tension melted away, I knew it was guided by the Creator, the universe, in that sense it felt big and spiritual. It truly felt like my whole being - body, mind and soul - received a complete healing. Very freeing! That pull had been resolved, both in my body and between my genetics' countries and ex-partners' genetic countries. Pretty amazing!

When we feel pain in the body, our body is telling us "hey, something is out of balance." When we go deeply into all angles of why the body is in pain, we often find our life has been unbalanced, possibly our nutrition, relationships, job etc. We may realize that we have just worked too much and not taken care of our health, we may have focused so much on other people or animals that we have forgotten to focus on ourselves, had too much caffeine or alcohol for a long time...

EVERYTHING is connected! The visible and invisible, our inner being and our relationships with others.

Instant healings ARE possible. If an instant healing is not happening, there are great reasons for that. We still need to learn something - there is still an opportunity to grow. It is so empowering to see it as an opportunity rather than punishment, a chore, burden or drag.

Physical Exercises to Heal Your Body

As you know, every body is unique. The following physical tools are very helpful for my body and may help you as well.

As with all tools, there is nothing like direct experience. This will allow you to discern whether they help you or other tools may be more beneficial.

Always listen to your own body.

Consistent practice for several weeks is often necessary to feel the benefits.

Tools for Scoliosis, Back and Hip Imbalances

Road biking

Benefits: Can provide pain relief and pain management benefits for low back pain, knee pain, fibromyalgia. Also can create balance in the entire body.

It's important to note that road biking can also cause pain or discomfort in some individuals, especially if proper bike fit and technique are not used. Additionally, individuals with medical concerns should consult with a healthcare professional before starting any new physical activity.

It creates wonderful balance in my hips and lower back. Having the feet clipped into the pedals allows the pulling up and pushing down to be balanced. Afterwards I feel like I have a new, balanced body. Really amazing. I do not get that same balance on other types of bikes when my feet are not clipped in. I enjoy a road bike ride at least once a week.

Specific yoga poses

Triangle (Trikonasana)

Benefits: Reduces neck pain, improves balance and stability, reduces stress and anxiety, increases hip flexibility

When I tilt, I feel a pop and great release in the hip of the longer leg. Always practice postures on both sides, even if you feel the most benefits on one side.

Forward bend (Uttanasana)

Benefits: Can help with pain relief and pain management in low back pain, neck pain, knee pain

Practice: From a standing forward bend I roll up very slowly, one vertebrae at a time.

Running

Benefits: Can help with pain relief and pain management in chronic low back pain, knee osteoarthritis, fibromyalgia

This may sound strange because logically it puts pressure on the joints. I run mostly on a soft surface. It loosens up my hips and back. Maybe I experience the benefit because I have enjoyed running my whole life. It is very likely that the sense of freedom and joy I feel emotionally, creates freedom and joy in my body.

Leg circles

Benefits: Scientific evidence specifically regarding pain relief and pain management has shown benefits of leg circles, as a form of exercise, can improve flexibility and strength in the hips, legs, and core, and can improve hip osteoarthritis and low back pain.

While leg circles may not have extensive scientific evidence for pain relief and pain management, incorporating them into a comprehensive exercise program that targets the hips, legs, and core may help improve overall physical function and reduce the risk of pain and injury.

Practice: Making large circles with each leg while standing also creates a pop in the hip of my longer leg and a nice release.

Baths

Benefits: Epsom salt baths are often used for pain relief and relaxation, but the scientific evidence for their effectiveness is limited. Due to the relaxing nature, salt baths can have some pain relief effects from fibromyalgia, osteoarthritis, and exercise-induced muscle soreness.

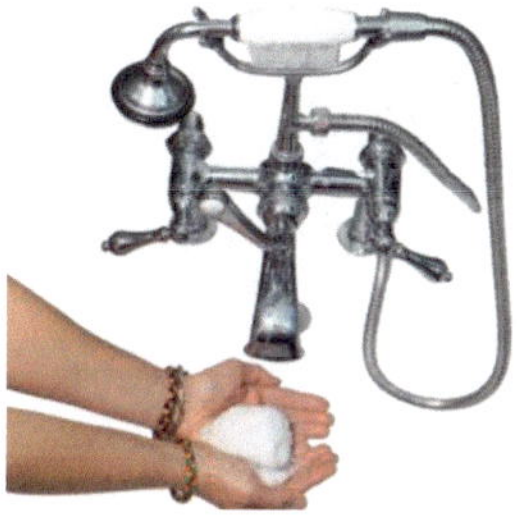

While scientific studies did not find significant pain relief benefits from Epsom salt baths, some individuals may find them helpful for relaxation and overall well-being.

However, it is important to note that Epsom salt baths should not be used as a substitute for medical treatment for chronic or severe pain.

Relaxing the body and whole being in a hot Epsom salt bath with lavender oil helps to soothe the whole being. After a few minutes I enjoy practicing a seated forward bend in the hot water, with knees bent or straight.

Additional Exercises for Lower Back Release

Imbalances in the lower back can be healed by strengthening or releasing the hamstrings, psoas and stabilizing the hips. Often the quadratus lumborum (QL) is tight and creates pain in the lower back.

The QL is the deepest abdominal muscle. It is located in your lower back on either side of the lumbar spine. It starts at your lowest rib and ends at the top of your pelvis. It is common to experience pain here because we use this muscle to sit, stand, and walk.

Causes for QL tension: To have better posture, many people while sitting at their desks, press their chest forward and butt back. This causes tension in the QL. Also leaning your torso to the sides while standing as well as sleeping on your side can cause tension.

The pictures below show the typical rounded back while sitting at a desk, which a lot of people tend to experience, the overcompensating chest forward and buttocks back, and the healthy position with a straight spine.

I invite you to notice how you sit at your desk and remind yourself to adjust your position to avoid creating stress and pain in your body.

QL (quadratus lumborum) balancing is a manual therapy technique used to alleviate pain and improve function in the low back region. While there is limited scientific evidence specifically on QL balancing, there are several studies that support the use of manual therapy techniques, including those that target the low back, reducing pain and improving function in patients with chronic low back pain.

Strengthen the upper part of your glutes

Lunges with your back leg slightly elevated on a platform. I am using a yoga block.

Side-laying hip raises

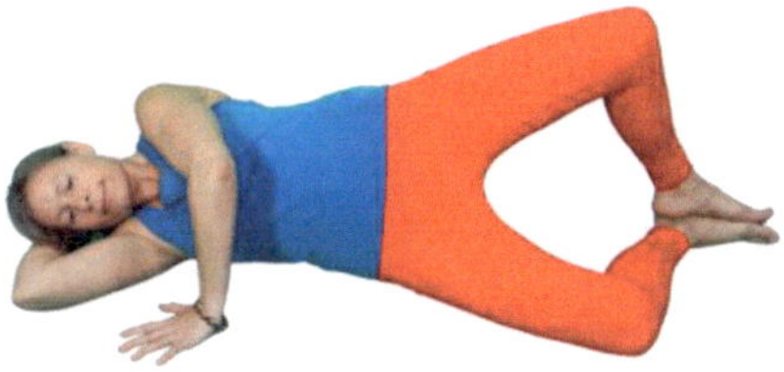

Laying on your side with knees bent, lift up your hips while abducting the top leg (lifting the top knee) with knee bent. Repeat at least ten times.

Change sides.

Bridge pose with strap (you can use a belt if you do not have a yoga strap):

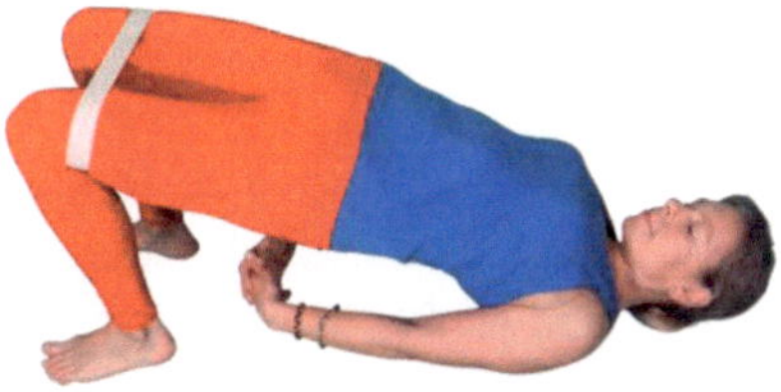

Lying on your back, bend both knees and place both feet on the earth. Place a loop of a strap around your thighs (the loop needs to be as wide as your hips or a little tighter), push your legs out into the strap.

Notice how your back feels. **Do you feel a nice release in your lower back?**

Sitting, have your lower back in a slightly extended position, but not hyper extended, shoulders rolled back, head on top of rib cage, rib cage on top of pelvis.

Lie on your back, place a tennis or lacrosse ball under the QL (on top of pelvis), move from side to side to get the ball in the right spot, hold for 30 seconds to two minutes until you feel a release. You can also roll up and down on the ball.

Sit on the floor with your legs in a straddle position. Reach with your right hand and hold onto your left foot with your left hand behind your left hip. Hold for 30 seconds to two minutes.

Change sides.

Kneeling with your torso upright, bend to the right with your abs engaged and touch the floor, then bend to the left with your abs engaged, and touch the floor.

Repeat at least five times.

From child's pose, move both hands to the left, hold for several breaths. Move both hands to the right, hold for several breaths. You can also relax your arms and form a pillow with your hands, rest your head on your hands, then move your torso to the right, hold, then the left hold, back to center.

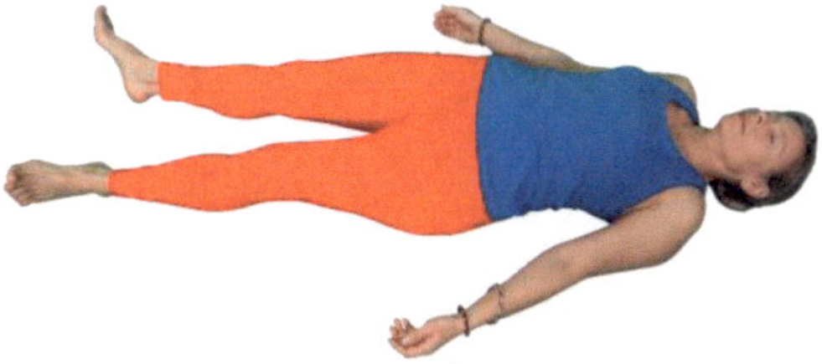

Sleeping on your back is recommended.

Hanna Somatics

Hanna Somatics, created by Thomas Hanna in the 1970's, is a type of mind-body movement that encourages physical and mental control over muscles that reduce chronic musculoskeletal pain. It teaches the brain to re-learn certain muscle movements to relieve tension.

One study found that Hanna Somatics led to significant improvements in pain, functional movement, and quality of life in patients with chronic low back pain. Another study found that somatic movement therapy improved pain, anxiety, depression, and quality of life in patients with fibromyalgia.

Overall, somatic movement therapies in general have been shown to be effective in managing chronic pain.

Hip and neck pain is often related to shoulder imbalances. Enjoy the following mindful somatic flexibility movements, and you may feel not just a release in the immediate area you are working on, but also in other areas of your body after a few weeks of regular practice. The more slowly you move, the more benefits you will gain. The illustrations may not show all details because a lot of the movements are subtle. Close your eyes and go within as you enjoy the practice.

Glutes and Hips

1. Lie on your back, bend both legs and place your feet outside of the yoga mat if you are using one. In a windshield wiper motion, slowly lower your knees to the right, back to center, then to the left. The slower, the better. Notice how each side feels, not stretching to the sides, just allowing and noticing how far your knees will come to each side.

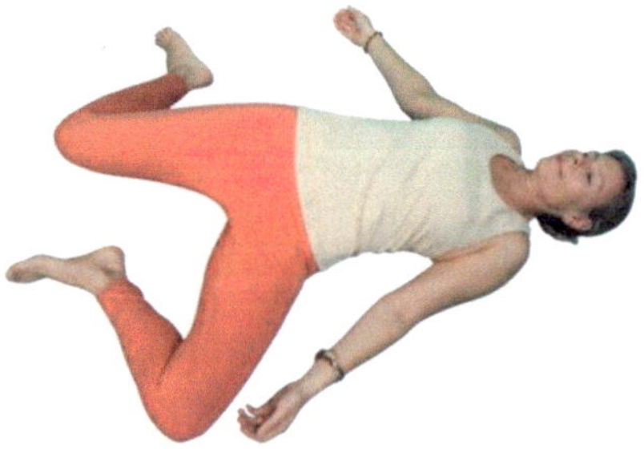

2. Lie on your back, place your left leg straight on the mat, bend your right leg. Interlace your hands behind the right thigh, breathe in and extend your leg straight up to 12 o'clock. Hold your leg for a couple of breaths, then slowly bend your leg while exhaling. Inhale and extend your leg to 1 o'clock, exhale while bending your leg.

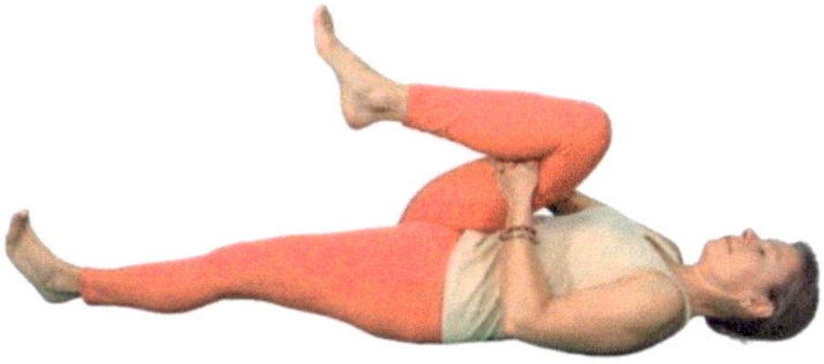

Repeat these slow, mindful movements to 2 o'clock, back to 1 o'clock and 12 o'clock, then to 11 o'clock, 10 o'clock, 11 o'clock, 12 o'clock, each time bending your leg in between. Slowly rotate your foot at 12 o'clock, exhale while bending your leg and straighten it on the mat.

Notice how this leg feels.

Change legs, and repeat the same slow movements with your left leg.

3. Lie on your back, bend both legs with your feet on the ground. Slowly lift up the right hip, then slowly lower it.

Repeat these movements with your right hip three times.

Straighten both legs on the mat and notice how each side feels. Bend your legs with your feet on the ground.. Lift the left hip up slowly, then slowly lower it.

Repeat these slow, mindful movements with your left hip three times.

Straighten both legs on the mat and notice how each side feels.

4. Lie on your back, bend your right leg, hold behind your right thigh and pull it gently towards the left shoulder, then gently press it away from you and lower it.

Repeat these movements with your right leg three times. Straighten both legs on the mat and notice how each side feels. Bend your left leg, hold behind your left thigh and pull it gently towards the right shoulder, then gently press it away from you and lower it.. Repeat these slow movements with your left leg three times.

Straighten both legs on the mat, notice how each side and your whole soma (body) feels.

Neck and Shoulders

1. Lie on your back, shrug the left shoulder to your ear, move your head to the left. Now, relax your shoulder, and move your head to the right.

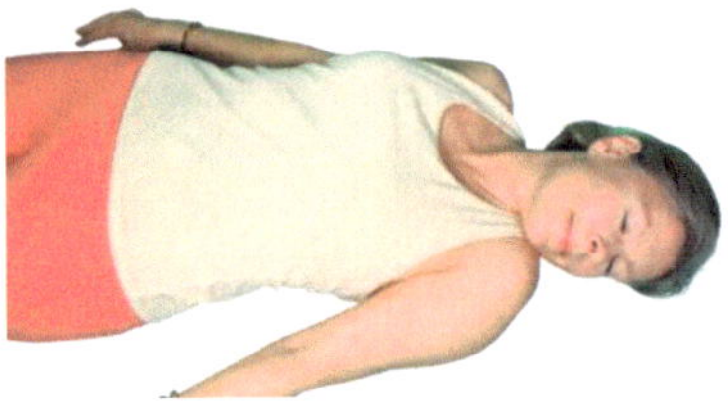

Relax your shoulder, and move your head to the right. Repeat the above at least three times. Then change sides, and repeat the slow movements for the right side of your neck and shoulder at least three times. **Relax and notice how you feel.**

2. Sit with both knees bent to the left, left foot against your right knee. Bring your right hand to the left shoulder and bring your head to the left, looking slowly to the left. Bring your head slowly back to the right while slowly looking through the room to the right.

Then move your upper body and head to the left slowly, and gently back to the right. Move your torso to the left, head to the right, slowly back. Move your head to the left, torso to the right, slowly back. Change sides, and practice on this side.
Straighten both legs on the earth.

Notice how each side and your whole soma (body) feels.

3. Lie on your back. Slowly press the right shoulder blade and left hip down three times. Then change sides, and press your left shoulder blade and right hip down three times.

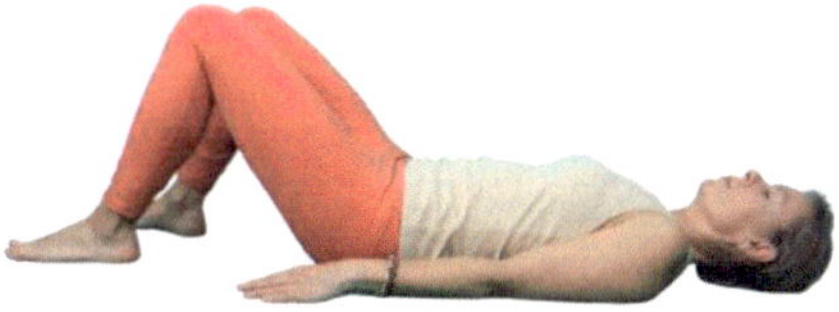

Slowly lift your right shoulder blade and left hip three times. Change sides, and now lift your left shoulder blade and right hip three times. Slosh your feet, with legs on the earth, moving the feet up and down, flexing and pointing. **Notice how you feel.**

4. Lie on your back. Your left leg is straight on the earth, and your right knee is bent with your foot on the floor. Place your left hand behind your head. Look left and press the left shoulder blade down. Practice very slow crunches by lifting your arm and torso to the right knee and right knee to your left elbow with your exhalation, crossing the midline. Inhale slowly back down, pressing the left shoulder blade down and looking to the left. Repeat three times.

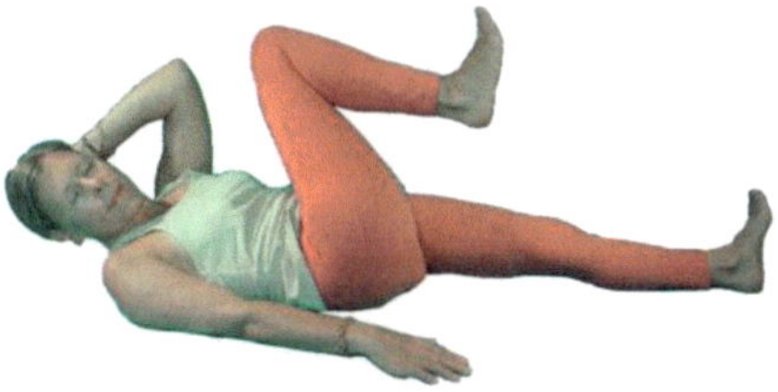

   Then change sides, and enjoy this slow practice on this side. Straighten both legs and relax your arms alongside your body. **Notice how you feel.**

Journal – How does YOUR body feel after practicing any of these exercises?

____

____

____

____

____

____

____

____

____

Heal Your Body Through Emotional Release

As I mentioned, people often hold anger in the liver and fear in the kidneys. The legs and feet are related to moving forward in life, the arms to doing, the hands to holding on or being attached to something or someone, and the heart to feeling love(d), forgiveness, and compassion when balanced, or hatred and sadness when unbalanced..

The more balanced your emotional state of being is, the more balanced your physical body will feel. Choosing joy, love, peace, and gratitude will greatly help your body to be healthy.

Self-healing gives confidence. Our body is a miracle, and it knows how to heal, it just needs to remember how and sometimes needs a little help.

Natural healing may take longer than taking medication, yet it is very empowering to know that your body has healed itself. We just need to remind ourselves to be patient and to trust the healing journey as well as the outcome and divine timing. Natural healing does not bring about negative or limiting side effects. It is our prana, life force that heals us.

Love, nurture and support your body. It is never selfish to focus on your own body, health and life. **I suggest the following affirmations:**

- "I love, respect and honor my body,"
- "My body is my temple."
- "My body, mind and soul are in harmony."

Feel free to choose your own affirmation that supports your health and well-being at this time.

To release stress, which can negatively impact your digestive system, breathwork is very useful. The **Cooling Breath (**Sitkari Pranayama) will cool down your anxiety.

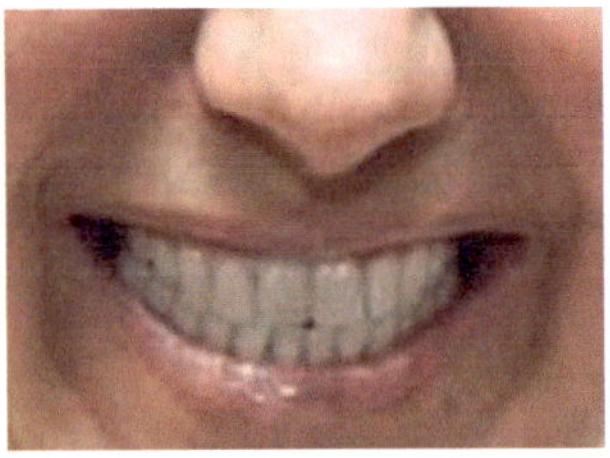

Bring your upper and lower teeth together while keeping your lips as open as you can. Inhale through the closed teeth, making a soft hissing sound. Close your mouth, and exhale through your nose.

Repeat for 10 cycles of breath, or, as long as you need to feel calm.

Physical Nutrition

It is also important to focus on healthy physical nutrition, which affects our brain and our gut (often called the second brain), whole body, and our life energy… really our whole being.

The concept of a "second brain" refers to the idea that the gut and the brain are intimately connected, and that the health of one can influence the health of the other. This idea is based on scientific evidence that suggests that the gut and the brain communicate with each other through a complex network of nerves, hormones, and immune system molecules. For example, stress and other emotional states can cause changes in the gut, such as increased inflammation, which can in turn affect mood and cognitive function.

If you do not eat and drink in an ideal way, you will feel heavy or spacy, restless, ungrounded, which will diminish your ability to focus and be present in the Now, and be efficient in life. **Serve your body, and it will serve you.** The choices we make for our health today make a difference now, in the near future and even in 20 years or more. Each choice builds on the next one.

Every body is unique. It is up to you to learn what is beneficial for you at this time. When they are young many people are able to digest just about anything. Our metabolism changes as we get older, and it is wise to adjust how we fuel our bodies to what we can digest and what will energize us in healthy, natural, balanced ways.

Reflect on what you eat and drink on a typical day in your life. Write down your current foods and beverages.

Current Breakfast:

____

____

____

Current Morning Snack:

____

____

Current Lunch:

Current Afternoon Snack:

Current Dinner:

Current Evening Snack:

Beverages:

Take a moment and journal how you feel physically, emotionally, and mentally about the food and beverages you normally consume.

Now look at the labels of those foods and beverages, and notice the amounts of added sugar, fat, cholesterol, carrageenan and caffeine. **Write those down next to your list above.**

Carrageenan is used to thicken, emulsify and preserve food, It can create inflammation, gastrointestinal ulcers and destroy the digestive system, so avoid it!

Even if you are not gluten or dairy intolerant, I suggest limiting or at least reducing both. Cow milk and wheat is highly processed in the U.S., and it may create inflammation in your body.

Caffeine creates an artificial high and energy. Too much coffee makes the body acidic, and depletes the adrenals. When the body is acidic, it allows illnesses and diseases more easily. Cancer thrives in acidic environments! **For optimum health we focus on alkaline foods and beverages.** Consuming caffeine after 2pm can also reduce the amount of REM sleep at night which is important for memory, emotional processing, and healthy brain development.

Just as you feed your mind with positive thoughts, **let the food and beverages you take in be your natural medicine.**

I suggest eating mostly fresh, organic foods without preservatives and artificial color.

If you often feel bloated and are experiencing inflammation in your body, some ways of nourishing your body that may resonate with you are "The Body Ecology Diet" by Donna Gates, "The Paleo Diet" by Dr. Cordain, "Eat Right 4 Your Type" (referring to blood type) by Peter J. D'Amo's and Catherine Whitney. There is also a lot of ancient wisdom in Ayurveda, which we will discuss in a little while. Your body is unique.

If you choose a diet that is mainly vegetarian, you will need to make sure you absorb enough protein - eggs, protein shakes, rice, beans, oat, coconut or almond milk, nuts and seeds are ideal options. Not every blood type can digest those equally.

Depending on your health, certain supplements help to replenish the body in addition to healthy food and beverages. This may be a multivitamin, calcium-magnesium-zinc (calcium is often recommended for women to strengthen their bones), vitamin C. For my body these are wonderful supplements. Look at your full blood panel, and see if you need more iron or other supplements. If I feel a cold starting I take extra vitamin C. It strengthens my immune system, and I feel fine.

The most healing choice we can make when it comes to physical nutrition is to eliminate sugar. Natural sugar in fresh berries is fine, but eliminate added sugar as much as possible.

Natural holistic cancer centers have in common that they highly recommend avoiding sugar, and they focus on fresh foods. The Nature Works Best Cancer Clinic conducted a study of 317 adult cancer patients over almost seven years. Regardless of the stage of cancer, those that did not consume sugar had twice the survival rate as those that consumed it. Of those that consumed sugar, 36% went into remission. Of those that avoided sugar, 90% went into remission.

You may feel perfectly healthy. I still suggest making a few modifications to your daily diet to stay healthy in the long run. To me life is about balance. Feel it out for yourself. You don't necessarily have to cut out all sugar, gluten and dairy, but reduce it to stay healthy in the long run.

What changes are you committing to to replace high sugar, fat, cholesterol, carrageenan and caffeine items with? Keep in mind that there are many delicious, nutritious gluten free and dairy free options available these days.

Some suggestions:

- Room temperature or warm water with fresh lemon juice before breakfast helps to alkalinize the body.
- Nuts are a great protein snack that contain healthy fats, which we need. They are wonderful food for the brain. Almonds help with weight release, they boost brain function and lower cholesterol. Soak almonds in water overnight for easier digestion.
- Fermented foods boost beneficial bacteria in the gut.
- Berries are high in antioxidants and provide a healthy snack.
- Lots of leafy greens will nourish your whole body, mind, spirit and soul.
- Cucumber can lower blood pressure.
- Carrots are healthy for the eyes.
- Xylitol and monk fruit are sugar free sweeteners that do not spike the insulin level. Even diabetics can use those sweeteners. I love them, also because they taste just like regular sugar with no weird aftertaste.

Combining the right foods is important for a healthy digestive system.

- Eat fruit on an empty stomach.

- Do not combine proteins with starches.
- Avoid combining different proteins.
- Avoid combining starches with acidic foods.

Ayurveda

Ayurveda is the sister science of yoga and is called the science of life. It is derived from the Sanskrit words *āyus*, "life" or "longevity", and *veda*, "knowledge", translated as "knowledge of life and longevity". It originated over 3000 years ago in what is now referred to as India, making it one of the oldest holistic medical systems. It remains as applicable today as ever before.

This natural approach is based on the fact that this world is made up of five elements, air, space,. fire, water, and earth. These elements are also what constitutes every cell in our bodies. We each have doshas, or body constitutions, that are influenced by these elements.

- **Vata** is characterized by the mobile nature of wind (air).
- **Pitta** embodies the transformative energy of fire.
- **Kapha** reflects the binding nature of water energy.

All three doshas can be found in each person. Many times one is stronger than the others, and through foods and lifestyle the doshas can be pacified, so that the physical, mental, emotional and spiritual body is supported and nurtured in healthy ways.

When I follow an ayurvedic diet I feel healthy, my body and mind feels calm, focused and balanced with no cravings.

Dosha	Element	Qualities
Vata	Air/Ether	Dry, light, rough, cold, mobile, clear
Pitta	Fire/Water	Hot, sharp, light, liquid, oily
Kapha	Water/Earth	Heavy, slow, cold, soft, steady

Vata:
People with a Vata dosha are usually slim, energetic, creative, can have poor circulation (cold hands and feet), and can get easily distracted and anxious. To balance Vata, warm foods and beverages are recommended. I like to drink warm water throughout the day. A pinch of cumin in warm water can be especially warming and grounding.

Pitta:
Those with a Pitta dosha are usually muscular, athletic, have quick metabolism and can be tenacious leaders. They are prone to inflammation and impatience. Cooling foods are helpful to pacify Pitta, but no iced beverages.

Kapha:
People with a Kapha dosha are usually strong and caring, provide a support system for people, and go through life in a slow, deliberate manner. They are prone to weight gain. Light and warm foods are beneficial to balance Kapha.

www.BanyanBotanicals.com is a wonderful resource for Ayurveda profiles and explains the different doshas in more detail, offers a dosha quiz to find out what your main dosha is, and suggests foods and lifestyles that are beneficial for each dosha as well as foods to be reduced for a healthy body, mind and life.

Discerning What is Healthy… for You!

Now that we have explored some foundational concepts, it is important to remember that every body is unique. Listen to your body as it tells you what it needs. Do not listen to your mind to tell you what you need. Your mind gets used to the routine, "feeds" into your taste buds and sugar addiction and may tell you "You know you want this sugary dessert. It tastes so delicious." When you ask your body, it will tell you "Don't feed me that. It doesn't serve me." It is your opportunity to find what is beneficial for you at this time. As I often say, "You get to learn it, rather than "You have to…"!

How do you know if your mind or body is talking? When you are considering eating something, close your eyes, take a few deep breaths through your nose to calm your mind, then say out loud or silently "Body, is this in my highest and best interest?" Listen to the answer. You may hear it as a "yes" or "no" or possibly "not now". You may feel the answer, a restrictive feeling means it is not serving you; an expansive, free feeling means it is serving you.

We used kinesiology, muscle testing, in the Affirmations & ThetaHealing chapter. Just as you can muscle test what limiting beliefs you are holding, you can also muscle test the food or beverage you are considering consuming.

As you already know, you need to be hydrated for this tool to work consistently. To be hydrated, drink a glass of water, ideally alkaline water. If you already had one cup of coffee, drink two glasses of water, as coffee dehydrates the body.

- Stand up, close your eyes, and say "yes" out loud. Without consciously moving your body, you will notice that your body will move forward.
- Close your eyes and say "no" out loud. Without consciously moving your body, you will notice that your body will move back.

Now that you have established a clear yes and no, you can test a specific food or beverage item that you are considering buying or consuming. Here is an example.

- Think about the milk you are considering drinking. Stand up, close your eyes and say "this milk is in my highest and best interest".
- Notice if your body moves forward or back. If it moves forward, it is in your highest and best interest at this time. If your body moves back, it is not in your highest and best interest.

If you do not fully trust your body or the response you are receiving from your body, or wonder if your mind is influencing it, add "without my mind influencing it", or whichever words resonate with you that will allow your body to show you the answer.

Based on this knowledge you can adapt your food and beverage choices to fuel your body in the healthiest ways.

Just because people say certain foods are good for you does not mean they are. Many people are very eager to suggest foods to you that they believe in. It may be healthy for them, but not necessarily for you. Your body knows best.

Keep in mind that sometimes the way that food is prepared can make a big difference.

For example, raw kale may not be beneficial for you; steamed kale may be. Turmeric powder may not be beneficial for you; cooked turmeric with some black pepper may be. Raw almonds may not be beneficial for you; almonds soaked in water for a few hours may be.

Without muscle testing it can be confusing and overwhelming to figure out what is actually healthy for your body. There may be a whole shelf of vitamin C in the store. Which one is in your highest and best interest that you can absorb in your highest and best way at this time? I strongly encourage you to use muscle testing as a powerful tool to determine what is best for you.

Make your list of new, healthy options below.

New Healthy Breakfast:

____

____

____

____

New Healthy Morning Snack:

____

____

____

New Healthy Lunch:

____

____

____

____

New Healthy Afternoon Snack:

____

____

____

New Healthy Dinner:

New Healthy Evening Snack: (Do you really need one?)

Healthy Beverages:

JOURNAL

I Need to Lose Weight

A lot of people say, "I need to lose weight." First of all, if you lose it, you may find it again. Let's change this phrase to "I am choosing to release weight permanently." You may have tried exercising more, dieting, doing all the "right" things, and you are still not at your ideal weight, meaning healthy weight with a healthy body.

You may have **limiting beliefs** attached to access weight or fat, such as these:

- "I am heavy."
- "I am overweight."
- "I will never release weight.
- "I am fat."
- "I need to hold on to the weight to feel protected."
- "I feel safe when I am big."
- "I am powerful when I am big or fat."
- "Thin and beautiful people are superficial."
- "I need unhealthy comfort food to feel comfortable and relaxed."

Do any of them ring true to you? You no longer need to hold on to these limiting beliefs, even if they were passed down by your parents, grandparents, or other ancestors. Breathe them out, and let them go completely.

Affirm these positive, supporting beliefs instead:

- "I look good."
- "I am thin and healthy."
- "I release excess weight and fat with ease and grace."
- "I love myself."
- "I love my body."
- "I am beautiful."
- "I am safe when I am thin and beautiful."
- "I am smart when I am thin and beautiful."
- "I accept my body, and let go of excess weight with ease, grace and joy."

Breathwork to increase your metabolism

To increase your metabolism and let go of weight naturally, the **Bellows Breath** (Bhastrika Pranayama) can be helpful.

Inhale through your nose, exhale forcefully as you draw your belly towards your spine. Inhale forcefully as you extend your belly out. Exhale forcefully as you draw your belly towards your spine. If you get light headed at any point, stop the practice, and return to your regular breath through your nose. If it feels right for your body, repeat this practice for 10 cycles of breath.

After your last forceful inhalation retain your breath for a moment, then exhale softly, and return to your regular breath through your nose. **Notice how you feel.**

What Your Food Cravings Really Mean

If you have cravings, your body is asking you for nutrients that are in the food or beverage that you are craving.

What you are really craving is not chocolate, chips etc., but rather minerals, vitamins or electrolytes that these foods contain. If you are craving sweets, you may actually be looking for the sweetness of life, not just sugar.

If you crave chocolate, what your body really needs is magnesium. The healthy foods that offer it are raw nuts and seeds, legumes and fruits.

When you reach for that morning cup of coffee, you may be missing phosphorus, which is found in chicken, beef, fish, eggs, etc., or sulfur, which is in egg yolks, red peppers and garlic, or perhaps iron, which is in seaweed, spinach, poultry and black cherries.

Are you hungry for oily snacks? You may need calcium, and you can find it in broccoli, kale and cheese, including non-dairy, almond based cheese.

A helpful and eye opening tool is Dr. Colleen Huber's food craving chart below. This chart breaks down the most popular cravings, explaining what nutrient(s) the body is actually pining for and presenting several healthy food options that contain it.

What You Crave	What You Need	Healthier Foods That Contain This
Chocolate	Magnesium	Raw nuts, seeds, legumes, fruit
Sweets	Chromium	Broccoli, grapes, cheese, dried beans, calves liver, chicken
	Carbon	Fresh fruit
	Phosphorus	Chicken, beef, liver, poultry, fish, eggs, dairy, nuts, legumes, grains
	Sulfur	Cranberries, horseradish, cruciferous vegetables, kale, cabbage
	Tryptophan	Cheese, liver, lamb, raisins, sweet potatoes, spinach
Bread	Nitrogen	Fish, meat, nuts, beans
Oily snacks, fatty foods	Calcium	Mustard and turnip greens, broccoli, kale, legumes, cheese, sesame
Coffee or tea	Phosphorus	Chicken, beef, liver, poultry, fish, eggs, dairy, nuts, legumes
	Sulfur	Egg yolks, red peppers, garlic, onion, cruciferous vegetables
	Salt	Sea salt, apple cider vinegar
	Iron	Meat, poultry, fish, seaweed, greens, black cherries
Alcohol	Protein	Meat, poultry, seafood, dairy, nuts,
	Avenin	Granola, oatmeal
	Calcium	Mustard and turnip greens, broccoli, kale, legumes, cheese, sesame
	Glutamine	Supplement glutamine powder to help withdrawal, raw cabbage juice
	Potassium	Seaweed, Swiss chard, spinach, avocado, sweet potatoes, bok choy, bananas
Chewing ice	Iron	Meat, fish, poultry, seaweed, greens, red beets, black cherries
Burned food	Carbon	Fresh fruit

Soda and other carbonated drinks	Calcium	Mustard and turnip greens, broccoli, kale, legumes, cheese, sesame
Salty foods	Chloride	Raw goat milk, fish, unrefined sea salt
Acidic foods	Magnesium	Raw nuts and seeds, legumes, fruit
Preference for liquids rather than solids	Water	Flavor water with lemon or lime. Drink 8-10 glasses of water per day
Preference for solids rather than liquids	Water	You may be dehydrated. Flavor water with lemon or lime. Drink 8-10 glasses of water per day
Cool drinks	Manganese	Walnuts, almonds, pecans, pineapple, blueberries
Premenstrual Cravings	Zinc	Red meat, seafood, leafy vegetables, root vegetables
Overeating	Silicone	Nuts, seeds; avoid refined starches
	Tryptophan	Cheese, liver, lamb, raisins, sweet potato, spinach
	Tyrosine	Vitamin C supplements or orange, green and red fruit and vegetables
Lack of appetite	Vitamin B1	Vitamin B1, nuts, seeds, bean, liver and organ meats
	Vitamin B3	Tuna, halibut, beef, chicken, turkey, pork, seeds and legumes
	Manganese	Walnuts, almonds, pecans, pineapple, blueberries
	Chloride	Raw goat milk, unrefined sea salt
Tobacco	Silicone	Nuts, seeds; avoid refined starches
	Tyrosine	Vitamin C supplements or orange, green and red fruit and vegetables

* **https://NatureWorksBest.com/naturopathy-works/food-cravings/**

Write down what you crave, and what healthy choices you will commit to.

Craving	Healthy Choice

Regular, Fun Exercise

"No pain, no gain." Do you choose this restrictive, self-limiting reality, or do you choose a joyful, uplifting reality, such as "I exercise with joy and see positive results." and "No pain, all gain?"

Exercise in a way that is fun for you! Vary it to not just use different muscle groups, experience cardio, strength and flexibility exercises, but also to have fun. You won't stick to your exercise plan if it is rigid and boring.

Mix it up; take 2 yoga classes a week at a yoga studio, gym or at home, go for a brisk walk, run or bike ride in nature, enjoy your favorite weightlifting workout in the gym or at home, practice Pilates, take a Zumba or Jazzercise class, or swim.

What exercises are you committing to and how many times a week?

Exercise	Commit to How Often (day/week)

Be present while you exercise. Leave your phone at home or in the car, focus on your breath which activates the movement of your body, be in the moment, take in nature sounds, make your workout a meditation in motion. **Enjoy!**

If you are not enjoying your exercise, affirm:

- ❖ "I enjoy exercising." or "I love my workouts."

If you need to motivate yourself to exercise, affirm:

- ❖ "My exercise keeps me strong and healthy." or whatever else motivates you.
- ❖ "I am committed to my health."

Feel out if you are energized and committed to exercise by yourself or with others.

After you have enjoyed your new diet and regular exercise for two months, reflect on how you feel.

____

____

____

____

____

____

____

____

____

____

Yogananda taught that there is nothing better than direct experience. Commit to the changes you noted because you know that you deserve to feel healthy and energized in a natural, balanced way. Make your healthy diet and exercise your new normal, your new habit.

After a few weeks you will notice that your body and mind feel less restless, more calmly energized without extreme highs and lows. And, along the way, you will naturally release excess weight that no longer serves you.

"I will reason,
I will will,
I will act,
but guide thou
my reason, will and
activity
to the right path in
everything."

Paramhansa Yogananda

Sixth Key - Passion & Purpose

"Be the change you want to see in the world."

Mahatma Gandhi

How can you live your life to the fullest? What does it mean to you personally to be fully alive rather than just surviving? What will you commit to that makes you feel fully alive? For some people it is being in the ocean, for others it may be riding a bicycle, watching a sunset, dinner with loved ones, playing sports, career, spending time with animals, traveling...

List 4 actions in the table below that you love, that make you feel fully alive, and that you can commit to regularly. Be specific.

Action	Commit to How Often (day/week)

You may get busy. Responsibilities may seem to want to get in the way of your commitment to these actions that make you feel fully alive. We only have this present moment. Each one of us deserves to be happy and fulfilled. When you get busy and think you do not have time to do what you love, remind yourself that you are worthy of being happy and fully alive. Take care of your responsibilities and set a specific time aside for your passions.

Love what you do, and do what you love. Bring love into every thought, choice and activity. Believe, know and trust that doing healthy activities that you love will fuel your body, mind, spirit and soul for the whole day.

When you live your passions, you will feel energized, alive, it will boost your immune system and your joy will be contagious to others. It is not selfish!

You will be focused and joyful at work when you take the time to live your passions.

"Passion is a feeling that tells you: this is the right thing to do. Nothing can stand in my way. It doesn't matter what anyone else says. This feeling is so good that it cannot be ignored. I'm going to follow my bliss and act upon this glorious sensation of joy."

Wayne Dyer

If you get easily distracted or do not take time for yourself regularly, write an affirmation on a post-it and place it on your bathroom mirror. "I commit to living my passions". Name your passions if that keeps you more focused.

How do you feel while, and after, living your passions?

____

____

____

____

____

____

____

____

Do you choose a lifestyle that reflects this belief: "I have to work myself to the bones to earn a living." or "I work smart and joyfully and earn money with ease and grace."?

In Germany we have a saying "First work, then pleasure". Why would work and pleasure need to be separate? Why not bring pleasure into work, and experience pleasure while being purposeful and productive?

Release the above belief as well as:
"I have to get everything done before I can relax."

Breathe them out and replace them with:
"I create and maintain a healthy balance between work and play."

Let's enjoy some balancing breaths.

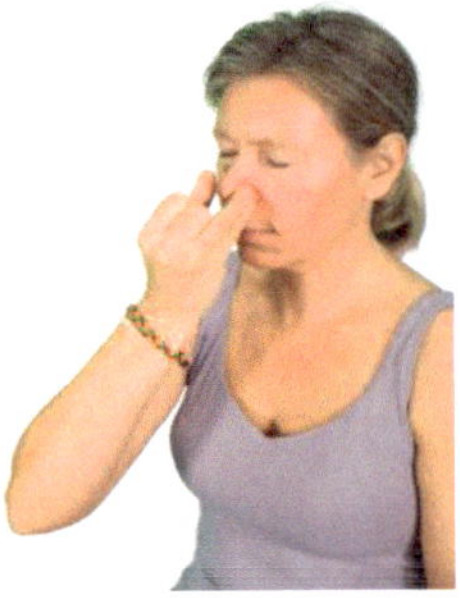

Alternate Nostril Breath (Anulom-vilom Pranayama) is a centering practice that balances the right and left side of the brain. This will help you to feel focused, clear and make choices with balanced intuition and logic.

Using your right hand, fold your middle and index fingers toward your palm. Place your thumb on your right nostril and your ring finger on your left nostril. Close your right nostril with your thumb and inhale through your left nostril, slowly and deeply.

Next, release your thumb and close your left nostril with your ring finger. Exhale slowly through the right nostril. Now practice it in reverse, this time inhaling through the right nostril and exhaling through the left.

Repeat several times until you feel calm and clear.

When you re-spark your spiritual practice, it will re-spark you.

Is what you like to do important to you because you think you should focus on it or is it truly a passion, what your heart is fulfilled by? If you are passionate about your career, is it so that you are able to provide for your family, or is the actual career your true passion? If providing for your family is the actual passion, write it down.

Your work could change to something that you are passionate about while still being able to provide for your family. **Journal your passions here:**

Spend more time enjoying those passions.

Your purpose reveals itself as you are living your truth in joy and gratitude. When you do what you love you are in the flow, in oneness with the universe. The universe is filled with unlimited possibilities, opportunities, and abundance - so are you. Trust it on all levels.

Doing what you love is not a waste of time.

Sometimes we may be attached to how we think our journey is supposed to unfold. This can freeze the energy. Once we detach and trust the flow, the energy opens up and we can be guided. Rather than taking action in a way that takes control away from God, we allow God to guide us, and co-create in a harmonious way.

Yogananda suggests living our purpose in the following way:

***"I will reason, I will will, I will act,
but guide thou my reason, will and activity
in my highest and best way".***

This is very powerful and meaningful. Once we align our human will with the Divine will, this guidance takes place, and manifestations unfold in a beautiful way, often beyond what we could have imagined.

Below are some helpful questions to ask the Creator before manifesting:

- "What is in my highest and best interest with respect to the people concerned?"
- "What is my purpose at this time?"
- "How can I live my purpose in my highest and best way with respect towards others?"

Listen to the answers rather than coming up with answers in your mind.

Journal them here:

____

____

____

____

____

Needs and Wants

Let's look at India. When I am in India, I feel extremely inspired. Many people are poor, live in little huts, own close to nothing and yet are so happy. The love and joy in their hearts is expressed through their eyes. Do they experience hardship? Absolutely, probably much more than most of us. Yet they maintain their inner state of happiness and pure joy. What do we really need? Is what we want and what we think we need truly necessary and beneficial for us?

What is it that you want, and does it feel in alignment with your purpose?

Take some time to journal.

What do you feel you really need, and what is beneficial for you?

___

___

___

___

___

___

___

___

___

___

___

Now go back to what you wrote and re-visit. Reflect on what you wrote. Is each item that you want going to make you truly happy in the long run? Do you really need everything you wrote down? Maybe so, maybe there are items on your list that seem important at first glance, but when you feel it out, there is not that much depth or importance to them. Make appropriate adjustments. When we **simplify our life**, we become less busy, less worried and more relaxed. We move towards feeling uplifted, free and happy. Often less is more.

Feel joy in everything you do. Have fun! Release the idea that having fun is a waste of time and energy. Do something that is fun for you without guilt or shame. It will energize you and increase your happiness.

Other people will feel your happiness, so **having healthy fun is not selfish!**

If you have a choice to be productive and efficient or to relax, what do you naturally do? How do you feel when you choose that?

How would you feel if you chose the other option that you normally would not choose?

Do it and note your insights, feelings, and thoughts in the table below without judging yourself negatively.

Naturally productive or relaxed activity	Feeling when you choose the not so familiar option

When we balance out doing and being, we feel more whole and complete, energized and centered within ourselves and in our lives. If we always do and exert energy, we will deplete our mental, physical and emotional energies.

Ideally, we begin the day with some exercise and meditation, taking care of ourselves, before we go out into the world and focus on external work. Ending the day with a brisk walk in nature and a meditation helps to integrate the experiences of the day, let go of thoughts and emotions that no longer serve us, return home to ourselves as the peaceful being that we naturally are and allow us to sleep deeply and restfully, rather than processing the experiences of the day in our sleep and through our dreams.

Deep sleep is the most restful sleep. We can then wake up in the morning, feeling awake and ready. Paramhansa Yogananda emphasizes the importance of being actively calm and calmly active. When we take care of our work while staying calm, we are much more efficient and more able to conserve energy than when we are agitated, stressed and pressured.

Fun & Efficiency Affirmations:

- "I am productive and efficient while having fun."
- "I deserve to have fun."
- "I know what it feels like to have fun."
- "I have fun in responsible, healthy ways."
- "I choose to have fun."
- "I know when to be productive and when to just be."
- "I am still living my purpose when I allow myself to just be."

- ❖ "I enjoy being without feeling guilty, restless or ashamed."
- ❖ "I know when to exert energy and when to recharge, and act on this knowing."
- ❖ "My work is fun."

Before you create anything, make sure your chakras are balanced and open, so you are a clear channel of and for the Divine. Towards the end of this book you will find "Yoga for Chakra Balancing". This is a wonderful practice before making important decisions. Creations flow much more easily and gracefully in this way.

Co-create with God!

Time is an illusion. Do not force anything in life. Be motivated, persist with determination and commitment, and continuously go with your guidance. Sometimes something else is meant to happen before what you want to do can manifest. Trust the guidance, the flow without resistance or fight.

The universe is supporting you. **Allow it!** You know that you deserve the support.

Here are some of my personal experiences that uplift me. I am sharing them with you as examples, so you can reflect on what inspires and uplifts you.
As soon as my feet touch the sand at the beach I feel grounded and held by Mother Earth. I love that! Just as I love swimming in the ocean, laying on my back in the ocean in complete surrender, merging with the ocean, sky, nature, all that is.

When I take time to do this, my chakras open up, I feel joy, gratitude, awe of the beauty, power, and magic of the universe.

I love watching sunsets at the beach. It feels like a sacred time to connect with nature. Sunsets are such an amazing manifestation of the Creator! As I live in San Diego close to the beach, I have been blessed to watch lots of them, and I still perceive each one as awesome. Many times I leave my phone at home. When I get home I have messages on my phone from people requesting healing sessions. That's because I open myself up to the flow of the universe. I truly believe that they feel that open energy and are guided to book a healing session to open up new possibilities and opportunities for themselves and their lives.

I schedule healing sessions before or after that sacred sunset hour. As I know how much it nourishes me, I keep that time open for myself. It feeds my soul, my mind, my whole being. As some of you know, I am happy to give sessions later in the evening, just that sunset time is ME time.

How will you create time to give yourself what you want and need? To nurture your whole being? When will you do it?

Journal your thoughts freely here:

- Before you take action, say a prayer, chant OM, and meditate. OM is the power behind all creation. It is the vibration by which God brings all creation into manifestation.
- When you feel calm in your meditation, connected to the Creator, one with all that is, breathe softly into your heart center.
- Enjoy a few slow, calm breaths through the nose, tuning into your heart.
- Now silently ask your heart, soul and the Creator "What do I need (to know) at this time?"
- Listen.
- Be open to receiving answers in all ways without any expectation.
- A feeling may arise, maybe a word or phrase. Allow it to come from your heart.

If you are not hearing a response, ask yourself "What is important to me at this time? What do I want and need?"

Our heart can give us answers that are clear and pure. Our feelings are our reality when we are calm. The mind can create many scenarios, reasons, shoulds, musts, have-tos, etc.. Now that you know what your heart and soul need, silently affirm it while being in the deeply relaxed theta brainwave.

- Always state it in a positive way in present tense.
- If your heart is telling you "focus on peace", silently affirm "I focus on peace".
- Repeat the same affirmation several times until it becomes a part of you.
- You can now affirm "I feel peace" or "I am peace"

Make this your ongoing mantra, repeat it over and over again. Over time your conscious and subconscious mind will believe it more and more and choose the vibration of peace for your inner being and the connection with the external world.

At the end of your meditation, when you feel peace, ask the Creator "What is my purpose? Tell me in a way that I can understand at this time."

Listen to the answers and be open to receiving them in all ways. Journal them:

____

____

____

Now ask "How can I live my purpose in my highest and best way with respect towards the people around me?" **Journal the answers:**

____

____

____

Don't get frustrated if you do not hear, feel, see or know the answer immediately. Sometimes it will reveal itself later that day or a few days later.

Be patient. Allow the doing to come out of the being and the being out of the doing. Your inhalation feeds and glides into the exhalation, as the exhalation feeds and glides into the inhalation.

The Law of Attraction & Calmness Matters!

What do you think is important? What do you focus on? Why would you want to focus on inner peace, rather than forgetting about yourself and focusing all your attention on your house move or other external things and activities? What are the benefits?

Your house move (while forgetting about yourself and your inner peace and balance) or your inner peace and balance (knowing that the house move and everything else will go smoothly when you keep focusing on your inner peace)?

Commit to inner peace! That's the energy that you send out into the universe and through the law of attraction, more of the same energy will come back to you.

Practice focusing on your inner peace. Notice how you feel. At first you may feel agitated, frustrated or worried. Or do you already feel trusting, calm, and peaceful? **Journal your answer:**

____

____

____

____

Take 5 deep, slow breaths through your nose, making the exhalation at least as long as the inhalation. **Notice how you feel now.** You likely feel calmer, more trusting, and peaceful.

Just stopping your activities for 5 deep breaths will create a state of inner peace and calm. **Now tune in.** Which of the activities that you thought were so important do you feel are still important?

____

____

____

Many of us do so much that we never stop and ask ourselves what we are really meant to do from the Creator's, our higher power's perspective.

You may get caught up in the doing and exert an enormous amount of energy. In this case you give away energy that you may need for your own health and well-being. When you return to your activities from a calm state, you will notice that you will be much happier, more focused, and efficient.

A balanced, calm state means no high or low emotional spikes, meaning your heartbeat is stable, your heart, nervous and immune system and other organs are not stressed, and therefore your health is improved. Trust that the external will work out, in fact it will be a success. You will thrive, not just survive. You will get proof over time when you learn to trust this more and more.

"My calm energy creates amazing results in life!" is a powerful affirmation and truth.

Of course, you still need to take action, just differently and possibly other actions, guided by the Divine, that voice that you can hear when you are calm.

Trust and act on your intuition!

Paramhansa Yogananda reminds us that ***"The greater the will, the greater the flow of energy!"*** When you act on your guidance, follow through with willingness, will power, determination and perseverance!

As a society you are used to asking, "How are you doing?" … rather than "How do you feel?" You tend to make what you do more important than how you feel. Your self-worth often seems to be judged, increased or decreased by what or how you do.

In truth, you aren't what you are doing, **you are who you are BEING!** You are a spiritual being having a human experience.

Being is as important as doing, perhaps more so. When you create that balance, you create balance between the right and left side of your brain and body, as well as between feminine and masculine energies.

Our main goal in life is self-realization, becoming more and more awake, aware and one with the Creator.

Fear stands for...

False Evidence Appearing Real

Commit to Your Heart and Soul's Needs

At times you may feel afraid to fully step into your purpose. Fear stands for **F**alse **E**vidence **A**ppearing **R**eal. Don't buy into your fears! If you are present in the Now,

there is no reason to worry about the future or unknown. The more you trust the flow, the more the flow will take care of you, guide and support you.

Trust that you are whole and complete without fear that is weighing you down or keeping you stuck. What are you afraid of, and is the fear grounded in truth?

If there is a true reason to worry about something in your life, connect with that and take action so that your fear and worry will be resolved.

If it is related to a situation out of your control, go within by focusing on your breath and allow your meditation to create an inner calmness and peace, trusting that everything is perfect just the way it is. You can infuse the situation, the person you are worried about, including yourself, with unconditional love and light.

Commit to giving your heart and soul what they need, even if other people do not relate to it. Everyone's path is unique. Do you need time for yourself? Nurturing? Support?

Take action to satisfy your heart's needs and desires. Make that your focus, without neglecting your other responsibilities.

How do you feel when you honor and do what you need and want in a non-selfish way? **Journal your feelings:**

____

____

____

____

____

This is part of living your purpose.

Purpose Dissolves Pain and Struggle

When you stay committed to fulfilling your heart's needs, you will find that the original struggle you experienced will start to disappear. You are no longer feeding the struggle with limiting thoughts, emotions or actions. You have made the necessary changes in your mind and life, and you are focusing on uplifting thoughts, feelings and affirmation.

Through the law of attraction, what you focus on will expand. You are showing the universe that you are choosing peace, so the universe will give you more peace in return. When your whole being is filled with peace, love and light, physical pain can dissolve. Without physical pain it is much easier to live your purpose in a focused way.

Trust and act on your intuition, knowing that it is safe. When you act on our intuition, you take a step towards your purpose with every choice you make, every action you take, one breath at a time. While taking action stay tuned to your breath, as it connects your mind, body, soul and the Creator. Let all manifestations be guided by the Creator, co-create everything with the Creator.

Whatever you like to manifest, ask "Is this in my highest and best interest from your perspective, Creator?" If not, there is no point in manifesting it, even if our ego wants it. Trust the guidance you receive. It will lead you in the right direction. Follow your path. You deserve and are worthy of it. You are one with the infinite universe, one with creation, one with the Creator and one with all that is. There is no need to limit yourself in any way.

I ask this question many times throughout each day "What is in my highest and best interest at this time?" I love the addition "at this time" because something may be in my highest and best interest, just not right now. Stay present in this moment. Everything arises out of this moment. The clearer you are right now, the clearer all manifestations will be.

When we built the Palace (home and retreat center, which people lovingly call The Palace, as it contains many items from Indian palaces), we often thought "tomorrow we will do this", and had a clear intention of what construction project we would take on. When we meditated in the morning, most of the time we got clear guidance to first focus on a different aspect of construction. Even when it did not make logical sense to us we always followed that guidance. God knows a lot more than our little minds.

We surrendered to the Infinite, took action based on that guidance, and in miraculous ways the Palace came together, in ways that we could have never imagined or planned.

When we surrender to God, our life can be even more amazing than what we can imagine. **Trust that it's safe to surrender**.

Let go of control, surrender to the perfect divine plan, trust the flow with all its turns and rocks along the way, and believe, feel and know that you are taken care of. You are always supported, protected, nurtured and nourished by the Creator. You are never alone.

You probably thought that this Purpose chapter is all about taking action. It is, AND before and, as you take action, it is extremely important to use the tools described throughout this book.

It is imperative to act through Oneness with the Creator! There is no sense of separation, no taking control away from the Creator. Embrace harmonious co-creation with the Creator. The Creator runs the show, runs your life. Ideally you are clear channels of God's love and light. That's when you can fully live your purpose and be of service to others.

Remember that you can only do your best, then you need to surrender and allow the universe to do the rest. Surrender does not mean giving in or giving up. It means trusting that the universe has your back.

The following affirmation will help you if you are not sure when to be in charge, and when to let go and let God.

"I know when to be proactive and when to surrender to the Creator."

Living your purpose can mean having a meaningful conversation with someone. Smiling at a stranger, which can brighten their entire day. Opening a door for someone and letting that person go first. It does not necessarily mean you need to create something seemingly huge. It is very important to check in with yourself to realize if you operate from your ego or your soul.

Yoga, affirmations, our breath, and meditation keep you connected to your soul's journey and purpose, and that's all that matters.

"Thou shalt love
the Lord thy God
with all thy heart,
and with all thy soul,
and with all thy strength,
and with all thy mind;
and thy neighbor
as thyself."

Luke 10:27

Seventh Key - Selfless Service (Seva) & Relationships

"We cannot do big things, only small things with big impact."

Mother Teresa

Many saints agree when they suggest that life should be chiefly service. If you think that you need to manifest something huge to be impactful, you may never do it. You may feel overwhelmed, and not even start it. Many people have lots of great ideas. Often they float from one idea to the next, and never manifest any.

When you co-create one little thing at a time, take one step at a time, you can create a huge positive impact without getting overwhelmed.

When you live your soul's journey you practice Seva, selfless service to others. You shine peace, love and light from your soul through your body and mind out into the world. Self-love creates love for others. Self-nurturing, self-love and kindness towards yourself creates the energy, motivation and drive to nurture others. You need to fill yourself with positive energy first before you can fully give to others.

Taking care of yourself is not selfish. Sometimes guilt may arise for taking time for yourself to just be.

David Hawkins reminds us in his book "Power Versus Force" that when you live in the energy of pure love, you counterbalance 750,000 people who vibrate in lower frequencies, such as fear, grief, anger, and other limiting emotions.

Allow yourself to feel and live in joy, love, and peace, and change the world!
Changing the world begins by changing yourself.

Be in Joy, Love, and Peace!

Serving Others

Paramhansa Yogananda expresses a very powerful message in this way: ***"Kindness is the light that dissolves all walls between souls, families, and nations."***

Amma, a spiritual leader known as the "Hugging Saint" for her practice of embracing people to convey love and compassion, states that ***"Love is the only medicine that can heal the wounds of the world***".

Just as powerfully, the Dalai Lama states ***"Love and kindness are the very basis of society. If we lose these feelings, society will face tremendous difficulties; the survival of humanity will be endangered."***

Vianna Stibal, founder of ThetaHealing, makes the point that ***"The only way to heal this planet is through the high vibration of love and kindness".***

As you already know, this starts within each one of us. You cannot be kind to others if you are unkind to yourself.

The following affirmations will help you to be of service to yourself and others, in a nourishing way.

Affirmations:

- "I am motivated through inner peace."
- "I practice loving kindness towards myself and others."
- "I trust and act on my intuition."
- "I live without chaos, distractions and drama."
- "I am of service to others while taking care of myself."
- "I love everyone unconditionally."

Ideally, we love everyone unconditionally. We do not need to like everyone or agree with everyone, but everyone's soul is a reflection of the Divine - loveable and worthy of unconditional love. When we love everyone unconditionally, we practice seva.

When we serve others, let's do it joyfully while taking care of ourselves.

What will you commit to today that will uplift someone else? Simply saying "good morning" to someone, can bring a smile to that person and uplift him/her. Whether they respond or not does not matter. Serving means not expecting anything in return.

Make a note of your commitment for today:

____

____

____

____

Notice how you feel after you followed through with it. Can you commit to the same action tomorrow? And the next day? It can also be something different. Just remember to do something uplifting for another being every day. Set a "daily seva" reminder on your phone or put it in your calendar. It is just as important as a business meeting.

Love and light are the highest frequencies in the universe and can dissolve conflict, pain, confusion and struggle. Be guided by your inner peace, gut feeling and intuition rather than external circumstances, chaos and drama. **You no longer need chaos and drama in your life to motivate you to live your purpose and be of service!**

What would it feel like to be motivated from deep inner peace? Feeling calm and at peace does not mean being bored or lazy. On the contrary, calmness and peace is very energizing, and it is possible to experience those beautiful feelings in all actions. Relax into action, focus on your breath while being active, and take action out of joy.

Are there things that you believe you "have" to do that you dislike? What if you could feel joy in it? Nothing and nobody external can make us feel frustrated or happy. Everything starts within us. When you wash the dishes for example, feel how soothing the water is. It does not just clean the dishes, but it cleanses your energy at the same time, washing away stress and tension. **Try it out!** Wash the dishes while feeling the water and energy flow and record your experience.

My Dishwashing Experience:

____

____

____

____

What do you dislike and how can you turn those actions into positive, meaningful, peaceful and joyful experiences? Your breath can help you a lot. If you feel annoyed, frustrated, or angry, focus on your breath. Take a few deep breaths through the nose and notice how it helps you to feel calm and relaxed. The breath is a miracle and an amazing tool for balance!

Dislike	How I will turn it positive

Commit to being at peace and joyful in all your activities!

Through the law of attraction, the more you give, the more you receive. This concept is not only emotionally healing, but it also promotes balance in your physical body, as long as you do not deplete yourself. Selfless service does not mean that you need to sacrifice yourself. When you tap into the Creator's energy and use that to be of service, you do not deplete your own energy. If you feel exhausted after you did something for someone, you have used your own energy.

Empaths often seem to suffer, as they take on energy from other people. If you feel that you take on other people's energy, especially limiting energy, take a step back physically or imagine taking a step back to be an observer. It doesn't help anyone for you to be so involved in each other or each other's experiences that you cannot remain neutral emotionally and energetically. The practices throughout this book help you to feel strong and centered in yourself. Stay focused on your breath, as you communicate and work with others. Keep a part of your consciousness within yourself. **You matter as much as others, as much as the cosmos itself!.**

Relating to Others

The body is temporary, as you cannot take it with you when you pass on. The soul lives on. Why is it that you meet someone who you have not previously met in this life, yet you feel a strong connection, truly a soul connection with this person, and you sense that you know this person?

This occurs when you know this person, or shall we say this soul, from another place or time. It may evoke a sense of comfort to reconnect at this time, as the souls are familiar with each other. There may also be a conflicting feeling or energy between you and the other person which means that there is an opportunity to resolve a misunderstanding, disagreement or conflict from the past or present, to learn a lesson and come to a place of acceptance and peace within yourself, with the other person, and the relationship.

Any time you hold on to anger, resentment or regret you not only send negative energy to the person you seem upset with, but also out into the universe, and harm yourself. All conflicts present opportunities to let go and choose acceptance; true acceptance and peace, not thinking "I should accept it" with a feeling of giving up or giving in with a feeling of defeat.

It is not helpful to have a conversation when you feel hurt or angry. If you are holding on to any limiting emotions, breathe them out. Then, from a calm space, have an open conversation with the person who triggered you, if you still feel it is necessary and beneficial. Remember that nobody can do anything to us unless we allow it!

If you are upset about anything another person expresses, realize that this person is a reflection of you. Whatever you notice, seemingly positive or negative, is also in you.

How can you be in acceptance of the person, situation, and yourself? When you are in acceptance of what is, the conflict will be resolved either by coming to an agreement or you or the other person may no longer be motivated by this conflicting energy and one or both of you will move on from the other person.

There is a learning opportunity in everything! The following affirmations will help you to learn and complete the lessons.

Affirmations:

- "I am aware of the lesson."
- "I trust that I have learned it and it is complete."
- "I know that I have the right to move forward, it is possible and safe for me."
- "I trust that I will no longer need to repeat the same lesson."

When you experience a challenge, perceive it as an experience, rather than fully identifying with the challenge and making it a part of who you are. This takes a lot of burden and pressure off you.

When you are happy, others feel your happiness, and you receive more happiness! **Your happiness matters as much as everyone else's!** It is not selfish or arrogant for you to focus on your happiness. It will free yourself and others.

You create your reality, and you have a choice in every moment. Are you choosing peace and joy or anger and frustration?

Think of a person that you feel has "made you angry or sad", or with the wisdom you have gained we can say, a person that has triggered you to feel angry or sad.

- Why did you allow this person to trigger you?
- How did it serve you?
- What benefit did you or can you receive from it?

It may have motivated you to move away from the person or situation and spend time by yourself. Maybe it energized you to physically exercise as a means of letting go of the emotion. Did it push you to do something joyful for yourself? Reflect how the trigger and emotion served or could serve you. What did or can you learn from it in a beneficial way? **Journal your feelings:**

____

____

____

____

____

____

Once you have realized how it served you, you are empowered to maintain the benefit without needing the anger or sadness any longer.

Affirmations can be very helpful for this.

- "I consciously let go of anger and sadness."
- "I choose joy and peace."

Many people find it challenging to forgive. It is very freeing to forgive the other person and yourself for the conflict. Harboring hatred in yourself can eventually cause disease in your own body. It is extremely important to release hatred for your own emotional well-being and physical health. You may believe that the person will hurt you again once you have forgiven him/her. Forgiveness does not open up the energy for pain. On the contrary. **Forgiveness is healing.** It brings light and compassion to both people and the situation.

If you are still holding on to anger, grudges, resentment or hatred, I encourage you to let it go now.

Affirm now "I forgive this person, the Creator for allowing the challenge to happen, and myself."

As with all affirmations**, repeat this forgiveness affirmation at least 20 times**, starting out loud, then softening your voice and eventually repeating it silently in your mind until you fix it into your super-consciousness, believe it, and feel it in your heart.

When you feel forgiveness in your heart it has become your new reality, and you are free. Notice how you feel when you feel this forgiveness in your heart. The burden, heaviness and negativity has been lifted and you will feel relieved. Your heart, mind, entire body and soul is now filled with light, and the other person is free to shift into positivity in his/her own way.

If you hold on to hatred, it can over time build up in the body and cause cancer and other dis-eases, so even on a physical level it is important to forgive.

You are being of service to yourself and others when you forgive and free others and yourself from conflict. Make sure you surround yourself with uplifting people, so conflicts will be minimized.

Affirmations:

- "I attract uplifting people into my life."
- "I create and maintain healthy, joyful relationships."
- "I respect other people and myself."
- "I am respected by other people."
- "I co-create harmoniously with others."
- "I have the Creator's perspective, definition and understanding on whom and when to trust."

"When you are at peace with yourself and love yourself, it is virtually impossible to be self-destructive."

Wayne Dyer

Animals Have Feelings Too

Animals feel energy, just like we do.

If you come home from a bar or any place that serves alcohol, you may bring spirits home with you. Not the "spirits" that we refer to as liquor, but entities that attach themselves to you. Drinking alcohol often creates tears in our energy field (often referred to as our aura) and anything can enter our energy field.

When spirits attach themselves to us, not just you and other people can feel them, or a limiting energy, but so can your pets.

When you come home from a transformational training or workshop, your pets will feel your new vibration, and may need some time to adjust and adapt to this new energy.

Our healthy choices serve our animals!

Allow them to be with you. Sleep will help you and them to integrate the new energies. Animals have beliefs and feelings, just like we do. We can help them to feel loved, safe and healthy by sending pictures of the animal being safe, loved and healthy.

When they feel these nurturing energies within themselves, they can then feel them with us and in the external environment.

Journal any feelings you have on animals in your life:

____

____

____

____

____

____

____

____

Be in the Now

Expectations lead to suffering. Let go of expectations, of the idea of how people or situations should be. Everybody has free will and free choice. Nothing is set in stone. Everything in nature changes, so does everything in our and other people's lives. If you expect a certain outcome, you become attached to it and maybe even concerned about it and forget to be present in the now. If the outcome turns out to be different from what you imagined and expected, you feel disappointed, sad, possibly frustrated, irritated and angry.

You cannot control other people or the external world. You can choose to relate to others and perceive the world through the Creator's eyes of unconditional love.

You are meant to enjoy your journey, not just the destination, and be grateful for all of your experiences, for all that you have and all that you are.

Often people blame others for the unexpected outcome. Everyone is in their own paradigm and experiences. People often act from their own pain body or what they think is best for them, not necessarily for others. Do not take life too seriously. When there is a different outcome from what you thought, it is probably meant to be this way. You create our own life through your thoughts, perceptions, feelings and actions.

Take time to reflect. Who are you still blaming, judging or criticizing? It could be another person and/or yourself. How is it benefiting you to hold on to the judgment? What are you learning or could you learn from it in a beneficial way? Are you learning patience, acceptance, unconditional love or what else?

Who am I judging?	How does it benefit me?

This is a wonderful time to let go of all blame, judgment and criticism towards others and yourself as well as regret.

Accept the situation, and forgive yourself and the other people involved in those situations. **You will feel relieved and free once you have made the conscious choice to forgive.**

Reward yourself with a few deep breaths through your nose, breathing in forgiveness, breathing out all remaining grudges, sadness, anger and other limiting emotions, until you have let it all go. Feel that you are in an emotionally neutral space.

Congratulations!

You are now free from the burden, free to be yourself as who you are today, and you have freed others to be who they truly are today. You are now able to be present in this moment, for yourself and others.

It is wonderful to live without judging others and ourselves. Treat others the way you like to be treated. Ideally we love everyone unconditionally.

You do not need to like or agree with everyone's choices, but I strongly encourage you to strive to love everyone's soul unconditionally.

Paramhansa Yogananda reminds us that "There is no more liberating action than sincerely to give people kindness in return to unkindness."

Everyone is doing the best they can with the tools and experiences they have at this time. When you trust that they really are doing the best they can, it is much easier to accept them and their actions as "it just is" without attaching anger, frustration, resentment to them.

How do you relate to and communicate with others in general?

- Do you truly care about others, or are you so focused on yourself that you keep talking about yourself and tend to lead all conversations?
- Do you ask questions about the other person's life?
- Do you feel what truly matters to the person you are communicating with and understand this person?
- Or are you thinking about your own life, things you need to accomplish, while the other person is speaking?

Journal your thoughts:

____

____

____

____

____

____

When we learn to actively listen to others with an open heart and mind, with curiosity and true interest, we learn so much about them, ourselves and life, and we co-create harmonious relationships. Everyone is in their own paradigm with their unique beliefs, opinions, and experiences. When we remain the observer, there is no need to get angry because of a misunderstanding or difference in how we see the world. It is fascinating to learn about how others perceive life.

Conflict arises when people hold onto their own opinions, believe they are right and others are wrong, when they are attached to what others should say or do from their own perspective.

Allow yourself to be who you are and allow others to be who they are. This way you create and maintain healthy relationships.

Only you can make yourself happy, and only you are responsible for your life. Nobody else is responsible for your life, just like you are not responsible for anyone else's life.

That takes off a heavy burden.

Make a list of all the people that you feel responsible for:

Imagine choosing to help them out of free will and free choice, rather than feeling obligated to help them. **How does that feel to you?**

Let's help those that are ready, appreciative and open to our help, so it will be a beneficial experience for all involved. How do you know who is ready?

Affirmation:

- "I have the Creator's perspective on when, how and whom to help."
- "I know who is open and ready to receive my help."

When I visited a great saints cave in India, the energy struck me as being so clear. It didn't feel filled with overwhelming love or joy to me. It was the same energy that I feel from the Creator, the clarity of "it just is", beyond emotions, duality, judgment, should, hope and try. That is the most helpful energy to vibrate in, both for ourselves and when we connect with others. If we get pulled into drama, pain, or struggle, we cannot be of service as much as if we stay in a clear energy. **From the observer's perspective we can offer clear guidance.** In this clarity we can still feel deep compassion. Trust that everyone is on their own unique journey.

Vianna Stibal reminds us that when we care deeply about someone, we consciously or subconsciously give soul fragments, pieces of our soul, to that person or animal. Set an intention that all of your soul fragments are washed, cleansed and returned to you and those that you have taken on from others are washed, cleansed and returned to them in everyone's highest and best way. This will help you and the other being to feel whole and complete.

It's All About Balance

Do you believe you need to give yourself away to be needed, wanted, accepted and loved?

Reflect on situations when you gave yourself away, your truth, your time, energy, soul fragments.

- How did you feel during these times and afterwards?
- Did you perceive these experiences as uplifting?
- Did you feel energized or depleted afterwards?

Journal your feelings here:

____

____

____

____

____

____

____

____

It is wonderful to be of service, but not necessary to give up yourself, your feelings or your truth. You deserve as much focus, energy, time and joy for yourself as you expend for your work and all other areas of your life.

Reflect and journal on how much time and energy you give each area of your life, including yourself.

____

____

____

____

____

____

- What can/do you need to change to create balance and equal time and focus for yourself and each area of your life?
- What does it mean to you to feel balanced within your body, mind, spirit and soul, all areas of your life and other people?
- How can you create balance between duty and responsibility, and joy and fun?

Take some time to reflect, and commit to four actions that you will do that will create balance for yourself and your life.

1.____

2.____

3.____

4.____

When you feel balanced, others will feel it and be uplifted by it.

The right side of the body is the masculine, active side. The left side is the feminine, receptive side. Giving relates to the right side, receiving to the left side. When you allow yourself to receive as much as you give, you are promoting a healthy balance in your physical body.

How do you recharge yourself to maintain a healthy balance?

I enjoy a weekly slow flow ME time in nature. This means I put in my calendar "ME Time" and commit to it. You do not always need to make yourself available for everyone else!

I flow in any way that I am guided to at that time. It often turns out to be a gentle bike ride (it's not a workout time, it's a slow soul flow), walk as slowly as I possibly can, **stop to smell the roses** - literally, sit at one of my favorite spots to just be, enjoy an ocean dip, and let the soothing, inspiring ocean bathe me in its bliss.

At night I often enjoy a spa with amazing jets or a soothing bath with epsom salt and lavender oil.

What are you committing to doing to recharge yourself regularly?

Recharging Choice	How often and how long

Seva, selfless service, means not expecting or counting on receiving what you give in return. You give freely; what other people say and do is their choice based on their free will. Love and give unconditionally. The universe will take care of you and give you in return what you deserve and are worthy of. Trust that it will happen in divine time and ways, not always instantly.

Balancing Being of Service to Others and to Yourself

Do you feel and/or believe that you always need to be of service to others? How much do you do for others and how much for yourself? Note the estimated time.

Time for Self	Time for Others

Choose this belief and lifestyle: "I nurture myself while taking care of other people and things."

- How do you feel when you are of service?
- How do you feel when you are by yourself?
- How will you best follow through with what is truly important at this time from the Creator's perspective?

Journal your feelings here:

You may have obligations, commitments, contracts, oaths or vows related to your partner, family, state, country, or government.

- Are these commitments still serving you today?
- Do they need to be tweaked or canceled?
- Do you motivate your partner by creating conflict and pain in his/her life?
- Are you motivated by conflict or pain?
- Is the pain or conflict still serving you?

It is your choice! Remember, you create your reality and life.

Compassion is the way to love, and love is ultimately the way to health, happiness, success and peace. How can you motivate your partner or family in a loving way?

Take a moment to reflect and journal about obligations, commitments, contracts, vows that you feel you have made and that do not serve you any longer.

- Who are you without them and do you trust that you are whole and complete without them?
- What have you learned from them?
- Do you trust that all the lessons they brought about have been learned, are fully integrated in you and you are now free?

____

____

____

____

____

____

People often say that we cannot change others. By changing yourself you will often change others. **Breathe out and release:** "It's impossible for me to change others."

Affirmation: "I commit to changing myself, which will help others to change."

Be kind and loving to yourself and treat others and yourself how you like to be treated. That is a balanced way of being and doing, seva to yourself and others.

Self-Care

When was the last time you truly took care of yourself? Who are you really? What does your body mean to you? Is it just kind of there, does it feel like a part of you? Do you judge it in a negative way? Do you make everything and everyone more important than yourself? Other people, your pets, your work etc...

Affirmations:

- "I matter as much as my work and other people."
- "I am important."
- "I deserve what I need and what I want."
- "There is enough/plenty of time for others and myself."
- "Things will still get done when I take time out for myself."
- "I am worthy and deserving."
- "I am" (this is a very powerful affirmation, "So Ham" in Sanskrit, it truly expresses the power of being, existing, having the right to be, to need, to want, to be seen and heard.)

Reasons for Unhappiness

Unhappiness often stems from regret about the past, fear of the future, and disappointment related to expectations and the outcome. This may play out in all different ways in different areas of your life. The solution for all is to be here now, in acceptance of what is right now.

People get upset about all kinds of things and events around them. You often can't fix external situations and other people, but you **can** change your perspective and work on feeling acceptance and peace within you. Voltaire stated simply, yet powerfully *"I have chosen to be happy because it is good for my health."*

True happiness resides within your heart, and the external can enhance it but the external can never give you true, lasting happiness. There is so much change, everyone has free will, so there is never a guarantee to what will happen.

The more centered you can be within your own being, the more centered you will be able to remain in relationship to the external world, including close relationships with loved ones. Allow shifts in you and people around you to happen through positive intentions. Focus on your own happiness, peace, love, and joy, and inspire others through your own positive actions.

You are responsible for yourself, that's it. You can inspire and help others, but you are not responsible for their change and their happiness. Ultimately, the choice to make a change to feel good and be happy is theirs. And that is OK!

Given that searching for happiness in the external world will always lead to wanting more, creating expectations, attachment, disappointment and pain, you really need to focus on happiness within you.

Spending Time Wisely

Yogananda shared the following story. A philosophy teacher put golf balls in a jar, and asked the students "Is the jar full?"

They said "Yes." He added pebbles that fit in between the golf balls and asked them again. "Yes."

Then he added sand that went in between the pebbles and asked them again. "Yes."

"This is like your life. The golf balls are what is really important like family, friends, your focus on God. The pebbles are things that are less important, and the sand represents what may just be a distraction."

There is only so much time in a day. **How do you spend your time?**

____

____

____

____

____

____

Does it feel balanced? Is it too focused on work or play, on yourself or others?

Sometimes I am asked if I work a lot. My answer is "I could say that I work all the time or hardly at all", meaning that my yoga and meditation practice, ocean swims etc are in service to myself and others, as I ask during this time "what is in my highest and best interest with respect to others?"

The ThetaHealing and yoga sessions and workshops I lead, and the spiritual events we host, help others and inspire and fill me with gratitude and Divine love and light. It feels like it is all one.

Reflect on what you will change to create a healthy balance.

Do you know how to **create a balance of giving and receiving**, doing and being?

When you constantly give, you will deplete yourself and have nothing left to give. Time for yourself is just as important as time for others. Everyone needs time alone to recharge, and just be. It is not selfish, needy or arrogant to take time for yourself. It means practicing self-love and self-care.

Breathe out and release limiting beliefs, such as:

- "I have to give up myself or my life to be of service."
- "I have to heal the world."
- "I have to save the world."
- "It is wrong to take care of myself."

Affirmations:

- "I am of service to others without forgetting myself."
- "I matter as much as others."
- "I manifest a healthy balance of giving and receiving."
- "I have a choice in every moment."

Allowing Others to Help You

Are you allowing people to help you? Do you feel comfortable asking for help and support, even when you feel healthy?

Do you always help others and never let them help you? Just because you are strong and can handle life does not mean you need to do everything yourself. People like to help. Giving them an opportunity to help you can be a gift. Asking for support is a strength, not a weakness.

There are many people who love to help and "make others feel good". As you know, nobody can really make you feel good, unless you allow them to and are open to it. They can enhance the happiness that you may already feel inside.

When the spark is already ignited in you, others can help you to turn it into a big flame. Don't you feel uplifted when you help someone else? When you need support, there is no need to do everything on your own. There is always someone who would love to help. It is a strength to ask for help, not a weakness.

The following **affirmations** will help you to allow support in.

- "I deserve support."
- "I am worthy of support."
- "I know what it feels like to ask for help and support, even when I am healthy."

- ❖ "I receive help without feeling that I owe the person who helped me."
- ❖ "I trust that people love to help me."

What do you need support with and who do you commit to reach out to?

I need support with...	I will reach out to...

Now go for it! Ask for support in your journal below, and notice how you feel during and after receiving support.

____

____

____

____

____

____

You may have noticed that the people that helped you felt joyful. We all receive and feel uplifted when we give and receive help.

When you get Divine guidance to ask another person for help, do so with gratitude.

As you get more comfortable allowing others to help you, you will feel less burdened, relieved and happy that others care about you and your needs. This can relieve pain and tension from your shoulders, as you no longer need to carry the weight of the world on your shoulders.

It can be a joy to co-create. Trust that it is possible for you to receive help from others that is actually helpful to you.; you deserve it and are worthy of it.

JOURNAL

Integration - Now What?

*"Live each moment completely
and the future will take care of itself."*

Paramhansa Yogananda

Congratulations!

You now possess all **7 keys** necessary to **own your own joy, peace, wellness, and happiness.** Do you feel that you are in a happy, peaceful, healthy space? Congratulations! That is wonderful, and I am truly happy for and with you.

Celebrate YOU!

Now is a wonderful moment to affirm:

- "I deserve to celebrate myself and life, and I know how to celebrate in healthy ways."
- "I trust that I know what it feels like to feel good and be happy."
- "I stay committed to no pain, all gain!"
- "I deserve it and am worthy of it."
- "I feel good, and I am happy now and in the future."
- "It is possible for me to maintain health and happiness in the long run."

Commit to continuing to deepen your practice of self-discovery with purpose, love and gratitude.

There is a story of a Master who spent 6 hours a day meditating. When he was asked why he still practices this much, he responded "I feel that I am making progress." (Anonymous)

When you feel healthy and happy it is just as important to keep practicing these tools that you now know enhance your health and happiness. You are paving a continuous path of pain free health, peace, love, joy, and happiness, feeling more and more one with the Creator, and living your purpose.

At times you will need to peel several layers and look at different angles, different perspectives of yourself and situations you experience before pain dissolves completely.

If you are still experiencing pain at this time, I encourage you to reflect on what is something positive that you are receiving or could receive from pain. Close your eyes, and let it arise. Trust that you can have this benefit without needing pain as a teacher or motivator. Allow the pain to leave, as it is no longer needed to teach you.

You may like to revisit the 7 keys. They are a tool for life. Don't be frustrated, rather be grateful that you are getting closer and closer to health, happiness and self realization!

Paramhansa Yogananda suggests:

"Use every trial that comes to you as an opportunity to improve yourself. The soul's nature is bliss: a lasting, inner state of every-new, ever-changing joy."

Continue to feel what is in alignment with your truth and live your own spiritual path! It is unique, just like you are unique. How will you know what it is for you? You will feel inspired and uplifted by it. Your heart will tell you what path to follow. All you need to do is listen to your heart, and you will know.

Make these suggested practices your own. Continue what resonates with you now, and explore others that nurture your whole being. Once you have found a spiritual path and practice that resonates with you, practice it.

Make it your yoga, your union with your body, mind, spirit, soul and the Creator of all that is. Over time you will feel more and more centered, peaceful, one within your whole being and with the world.

Be committed to your path. Explore. There are beautiful crystal bowl sound healings online and maybe even in your area, meditations you can join, kirtans (spiritual concerts), prayer circles and other inspiring opportunities.

Make it fun!

What Life Can Teach Us

... and how we can apply these lessons into our daily lives

- Go with the flow. You can't control your environment. You CAN control yourself. Life teaches us to be flexible, trust that God has our best interest at heart, and we are guided. God knows what we really need.
- Type A personality? Let it go! Learn patience and surrender.
- Perfectionist? Let it go! You are perfect as you are, made in God's image. Stop judging yourself. Love your imperfections, do the best you can and know that is enough.
- Get comfortable with change and embrace it! Nothing is set in stone. Everything changes.
- Appreciate what you have. Clean water, air, environment, healthy food, and each other!
- Churches, temples, altars, incense, bells etc. serve as great reminders to stay connected and immersed in God. Peace is the underlying foundation.
- Noise (traffic, train horns, etc.) can cover up the peace that underlies it all. Keeping a chant going mentally can help you to stay connected and not to get distracted and pulled into external chaos.
- So much happens in the silence. ***"Be still and know that I am God."*** Psalm 46. Gazing into a sadhu's (holy woman or man's) eyes, the windows to the soul, can create oneness and peace when we are open to aligning our consciousness with hers or his. That's a very powerful soul tune-up and blessing!
- You don't have to sit in silent meditation all day to be spiritual. Just keep God in your mind and heart throughout the day.
- Be present in the Now. Enjoy this moment. Connecting with a deeply spiritual person's presence and feeling deep peace is such a gift. A minute later this being or you may walk on, ready and open to experience the new moment, rather than trying to hold on to the previous experience and freezing the energy of the new. Detach and enjoy the new experience.
- Be thankful and see, feel, know God in everyone and everything. There is beauty and magic everywhere, in you, in nature. Don't take anything or anyone for granted.
- Make your sadhana (spiritual practice) fun. Go for a meditative nature walk while chanting, listen to the sound of the ocean or river and become immersed in

it, and create your own personal relationship with God.

- Stay attuned to God, and everything will fall into place. God comes first, not squeezed in after being busy with everything else.

It really works! The more you do it, the more "proof" and positive results you will experience, and begin to trust it more and more.

After exploring your own path, what spiritual practice do you enjoy that helps you to feel centered, peaceful and uplifted? Journal it here:

"Seek ye first the kingdom of God, and his righteousness, and all these things shall be added to you."

Matthew 6:33

Gentle Yoga for a Balanced Life

"Yoga does not just change the way we see things, it transforms the person who sees."

B.K.S Iyengar

As you now know, yoga means union. Each of the practices below are opportunities to co-create union with your body, mind, spirit, soul, and the universe. They are designed to increase flexibility, strength, and bring peace into your body, mind, soul, and life. It is often said that yoga is a reflection of life. When you feel balance in a pose, you will feel balance in your life.

If you are pregnant, please do not practice poses on your belly or twists. If you have a yoga mat, feel free to use it; if you don't, don't worry about it! No yoga clothes required! Keep it simple. You may like to have blocks, or thick books, and a strap or belt available as props for some asanas. Most importantly, flow with joy, without pain and without expectations! Stay in a beginner's yogic mind. Every moment is new. Co-create ever new joy and peace!

- Breathe through your nose with the affirmation, as you allow your breath to move your body. One deep, purposeful breath is more beneficial than three fast breaths.
- Move slowly and mindfully.
- Coming out of a pose gently and mindfully is just as important as moving into one.
- I invite you to hold each pose for several deep, slow breaths to fully receive all mental, physical, emotional, and spiritual benefits. In physical therapy 30 second holds are suggested, in yoga at least five deep, slow breaths are often beneficial. Always listen to and honor your body.
- Soften the pose gently if you feel any pain. Remember, NO PAIN, ALL GAIN! Own your own pain relief! (do what works for YOUR body, mind, and soul in each moment.)
- If you are unable to breathe calmly, you have gone too far. Gently soften the pose and return to a peaceful breath. We focus on expansion, rather than restriction.

- Take time to notice how you feel without judgment. It is a practice of self-love. It is common that one side of the body feels different from the other. Allow and let your breath do the magic!
- The mudra (yoga pose for the hands) and pranayama (life force exercise) will enhance the life force within your whole being. With certain mudras you can practice the pranayama as you are holding the mudra. I invite you to practice each mudra for about 30 cycles of breath up to five minutes to receive the benefits.

"Mastery of yoga is really measured by how it influences our day-to-day living, how it enhances our relationships, how it promotes clarity and peace of mind."

T.K.V. Desikachar

Yoga for Balance

You are empowered and capable to create balance in your mind, body, soul, and in all areas of your life. To experience balance in your life you need to first cultivate balance within you.

Benefits: Balance of the right and left hemispheres of your brain and body, masculine and feminine energies, doing and being, giving and receiving. When you feel balanced, you will naturally attract balanced people and situations into your life.

Affirmation: "In the center of life's storms I stand serene"

Asana: Mountain Pose (Tadasana)

Stand with both feet slightly apart. Your arms are by your side with palms facing forward. Lift and spread your toes, then place them on the ground. Broaden your chest, and allow your shoulder blades to draw towards each other and down your back. Place your head directly above your hips and gaze straight ahead. Take some deep slow breaths, while mentally affirming **"In the center of life's storms I stand serene"**.

Benefits:

- Improves posture, balance and reduces falls
- Is often used as a starting point for other standing poses
- Reduces stress and anxiety
- Improves lung function
- Reduces blood pressure

Asana: Balancing Table (Dandayamna Bharmanasana)

Being on your hands and knees with hands under your shoulders and knees under your hips. inhale your left arm forward, thumb facing up, and extend your right leg back. Take three to five deep slow breaths through the nose, mentally affirming **"In**

the center of life's storms I stand serene". Exhale while lowering your hand and leg.

Change sides, and enjoy the same practice with your right arm forward and left leg back. Repeat three to five times on each side, enjoying deep, slow breaths as you hold the pose. **Notice how each side feels.**

Benefits:

- Builds core strength and lengthens the spine
- Improves balance, focus, memory and coordination

Chair option: Sitting on a chair, inhale your right arm up, while lifting your left leg up. You can extend your left leg forward if you choose. Hold the pose for three to five deep, slow breaths. With each breath mentally affirm "**In the center of life's storms I stand serene"**. Lower your arm and leg with the exhalation. Change sides and enjoy the same practice with your left arm up and right leg up or forward.

Repeat three to five times on each side.

Asana: **Dancer** (Natarajasana)

From Mountain Pose, standing with both feet next to each other, arms alongside your body, look at one point in front of you that does not move. Inhale your right arm up and take a few deep breaths. mentally affirming **"In the center of life's storms I stand serene"**. You can stand against a wall for support. Bend your left knee, so your heel moves towards your buttocks. Hold onto your left ankle with your left hand. This is a beautiful balancing pose.

If you like, you can slowly move your torso forward. The more you press your foot into your hand, the easier it is to maintain your balance. Take a few deep, slow breaths, and repeat your affirmation. Slowly inhale your torso up, exhale your arm and leg down, and stand in mountain pose. Change sides, and enjoy this practice standing on your left leg.   Notice how each side feels.

Benefits:

- Strengthens the feet, legs, core, back and arms
- Opens the front of the body and hip flexors
- Improves balance, focus and concentration

Chair option: Sitting towards the front of a chair, inhale your right arm up above your head. Bend your left knee, so your heel moves towards your buttocks. Reach your left arm back. You may be able to hold your left ankle with your left hand while keeping the right arm extended above your head. You may like to gently lift your right foot off the ground for a couple of breaths. Mentally affirm with each breath **"In the center of life's storms I stand serene"**.

Change sides and enjoy this practice on this side.

Asana: **Eagle** (Garudasana)

From Mountain Pose, standing with both feet next to each other, arms alongside your body, inhale your arms up above your head. Exhale your right elbow under your left. Your palms may touch or move towards each other. Maintaining this pose, inhale your arms up to feel a stretch in your shoulders.

Take a few deep, slow breaths. mentally affirming **"In the center of life's storms I stand serene"**. Exhale your elbows down. Bend your knees, wrap your right knee over the left knee. Your toes can touch the ground on the outside of your left foot or you can wrap your right foot around your left ankle. Squeeze under your ankles, ground, armpits, elbow and wrists to activate the lymphatic system. Take a few breaths, silently repeating with your affirmation.

Relax your arms and legs and return to Mountain Pose.

Change sides and enjoy this practice on this side.

Benefits:

- Improves balance and stability
- Reduces stress and anxiety
- Enhances concentration
- Stretches and tones muscles
- Boosts energy
- Relieves tension in the neck and shoulders
- Can help reduce stress and anxiety levels in healthy adults
- Can help reduce pain and disability in patients with chronic low back pain.
- Can improve physical function and quality of life in older adults with chronic health conditions.

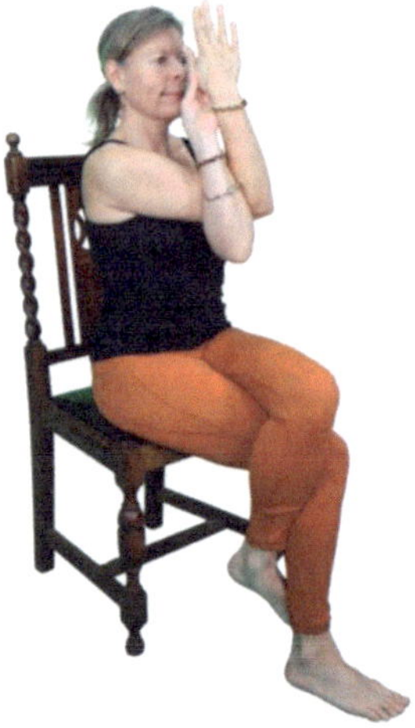

Chair and floor option: Perform the pose as described above seated on a chair or lying on your back. Remember to take deep, slow breaths in this pose, mentally affirming **"In the center of life's storms I stand serene"**. Remember to change sides, and enjoy the practice on this side as well to create balance in your body, mind, and life..

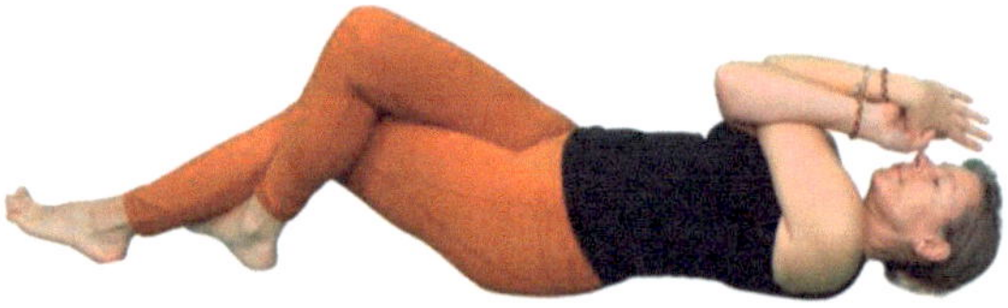

Mudra: Mudra for the Mind (Hakini Mudra)

Bring the tips of your thumbs together, tips of index fingers, middle fingers, ring fingers and little fingers and place your hands at your third eye, the point between your eyebrows. Mentally affirm **"In the center of life's storms I stand serene"**. Feel that your brain and body are getting balanced.

Pranayama: Alternate Nostril Breathing (Nadi Shodhana)

It is written that here are 72,000 nadis (energy channels) in the body which deliver prana to your cells. This pranayama will enhance the prana in your body, balance the right and left side of your brain, and purify your cells.

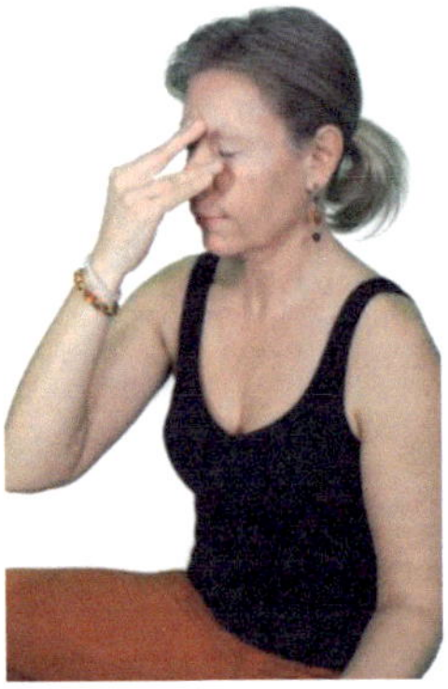

Raise your right hand and rest your index finger and middle finger on your forehead at your Third Eye Chakra.

Let your thumb rest on your right nostril. Rest your ring finger and little finger on your left nostril. Block your right nostril with your thumb and inhale through your left nostril.
Next, block your left nostril and release your thumb to exhale through your right nostril. Keep the breath out for a few seconds.

Alternate this pattern of deep, slow breathing from left to right and then right to left 10 to 15 times. Notice how balanced you feel.

Yoga for Believing

When you **believe in the power of the Divine**, and know that you are one with it, miracles can happen. Open to believing that you are a divine spark of God, and in that knowing, everything is possible for you!

Benefits: Opening to believing in unlimited possibilities and oneness with all that is. Believe that **YOU CAN heal yourself** through these simple yogic practices applied with intention (affirmation) and devotion (emotion).

Affirmation: **"I believe in the self-healing power within me"**

Asana: **Cat-Cow** (Chakravakasana)
Open all your chakras along your spine.

On your hands and knees with your hands under your shoulders, and knees under your hips. Inhale your head and tailbone up, arching your back, exhale, rounding in.

Repeat ten times, slowly and mindfully, while mentally affirming **"I believe in the self-healing power within me"**.

Benefits:

- Mobilizes and stretches the spine in flexion and extension.
- Massages and stimulates the spinal discs, improving spinal health.
- Releases tension and stiffness in the back, shoulders, and neck.
- Increases spinal flexibility and range of motion.
- Promotes relaxation and helps relieve stress.

Chair option: Seated on a chair, inhale, arching your spine, exhale, rounding in. Repeat ten times, slowly and mindfully, while mentally affirming **"I believe in the self-healing power within me"**.

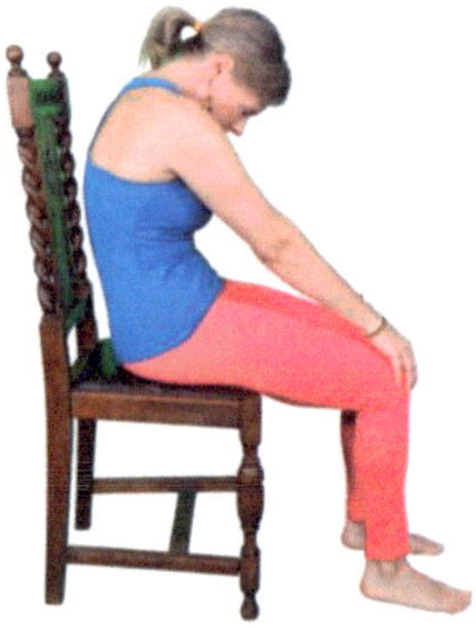

Asana: **Modified Table Top** (Ardha Bharmanasana)

From hands and knees inhale your right leg back with your knee bent, foot towards the sky. Hold on to your right foot with your left hand. Look back or up, depending on where your neck feels most open and free. If you cannot reach your foot, simply reach your left arm back (see 2nd illustration below).

Take a few deep breaths, opening your body, mind and life to the universe. Wish each breath mentally affirm **"I believe in the self-healing power within me"**. Slowly return to table top.

Change sides and enjoy the practice on this side.

Benefits:

- Strengthens the core, shoulders, and wrists.
- Improves stability and balance.
- Stretches the front body, including the chest and abdomen.
- Promotes flexibility in the spine and hips.
- Increases body awareness and mindfulness.

Floor option: Practice the above pose while laying on your belly. Hold on to your right foot with your left hand. **Hold your head down or lift** (as illustrated in the 2 pictures), depending on where your neck feels most open and free.

Asana: **Seated Side Stretch** (Parsva Sukhasana)

Sit with your right leg extended to the right. Bend your left leg and place your left foot to the right inner thigh. Inhale your left arm up over your head and exhale it over your right leg. Place your right arm on the inside of your right leg. Take a few deep breaths in this expansion, while mentally affirming **"I believe in the self-healing power within me"**.

Change sides and enjoy the practice on this side.

Benefits:

- Stretches the side body muscles, including those between the ribs.
- Increases flexibility and mobility in the spine and ribcage.
- Relieves tension and tightness in the shoulders, neck, and obliques.
- Stimulates digestion and improves circulation to the abdominal organs.
- Helps alleviate discomfort associated with prolonged sitting or poor posture.
- Promotes relaxation and a sense of openness in the chest and lungs.
- Can be practiced anywhere; a convenient stretch for relieving stiffness during sedentary activities.

Chair option: Extend your right leg to the right. Inhale your left arm up over your head and exhale it over your right leg. Place your right arm on the inside of your right leg. Take a few deep breaths in this expansion, while mentally affirming **"I believe in the self-healing power within me"**. Change sides and enjoy the practice on this side.

Asana: **Tree** (Vrksasana)

Stand with both feet firmly rooted into the earth. Look at one spot in front of you that does not move. Place your right foot against your inner left calf or thigh. Your toes can also touch the ground for more stability. Inhale your arms out to the sides, or you can place your palms at your heart center. If you feel stable, allow your breath to reach your arms up. Ground into the earth and reach up to the heavens. Take a few deep, mindful breaths, while mentally affirming **"I believe in the self healing power within me"**.

Exhale your arms and foot down.

Change sides, and enjoy the practice on this side.

Benefits:

- Improves balance and reduces falls
- Reduces stress and anxiety
- Improves joint position sense
- Increases muscle strength and endurance

Floor option: Laying on your back, practice the above pose as described above.

Mudra: Shiva Linga

Extend your left hand at your navel with your palm facing up. Make a fist with your right hand, and place it on your left palm. Extend your right thumb up. Enjoy deep, slow breaths as you hold this mudra, mentally affirming **"I believe in the self healing power within me"**.

This mudra strengthens prana and increases self confidence, which will help you to fortify your belief in your healing power.

Additional Mudra: Lotus (Padma) Mudra

Place both hands in front of your heart, so the edges of your hands and pads of your fingers touch each other. Open this bud of the lotus flower by opening up and spreading wide your index, middle and ring fingers and palms. Only the tips of your little fingers and outer edge of your thumbs touch. Take a few deep, slow breaths here, mentally affirming **"I believe in the self healing power within me"**.

Then close the lotus bud by drawing your fingernails together and touching the back of your hands. Your hands point down to the earth.

Open this lotus flower when you are ready to allow more light and blessings into your whole being, close the lotus bud to go within.

Pranayama: **Three-Part Yogic Breath** (Dirga Pranayama)

This life force exercise brings fresh prana, life force, into our core, and creates balance in our solar plexus and heart chakras, digestive and respiratory systems.

Close your eyes, and gently lift your gaze to your third eye, your intuitive center between your eyebrows. Breathe in through the nose while pushing the belly out.

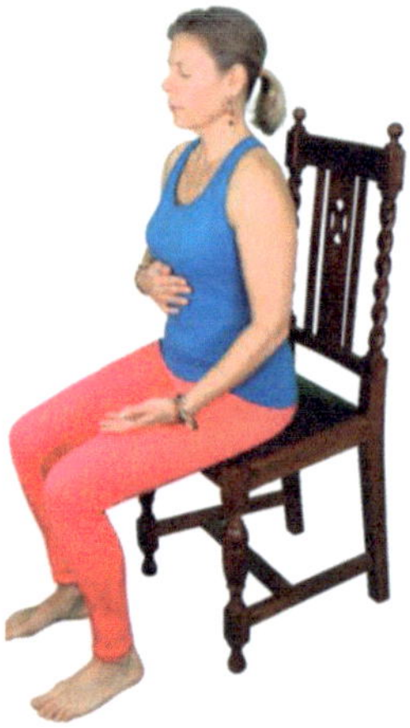

Draw the same breath into your ribcage, and into your chest while mentally affirming

"I believe in the self healing power within me".

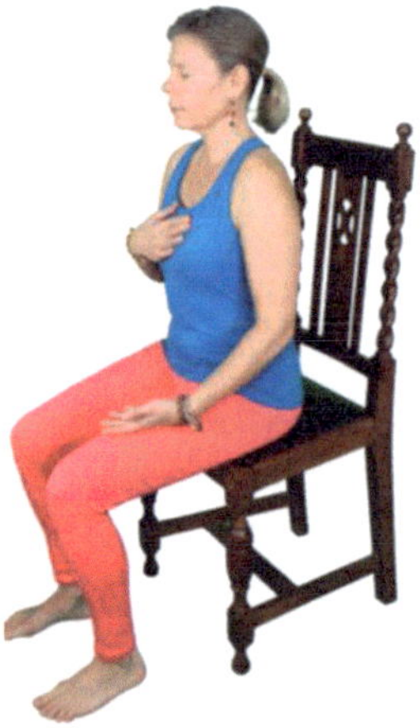

Exhale the same breath from your chest, then ribcage, then belly, draw your belly in towards your spine, breathing out fear, pain or whatever you like to release.

Repeat at least 10 times. Notice how empowered you feel.

Yoga for Compassion

To feel compassion for others, it is important to feel compassion and love for yourself first. If you care deeply for others but not for yourself, you may deplete yourself.

You are as valuable as others, and in fact, as valuable as the cosmos!

What one needs to feel compassion...

- Detach from all expectations and outcomes.
- Be present in this moment with an open heart to feel joy.
- Choose loving kindness towards yourself and others.
- See God in everyone.
- Recognize everyone as a beautiful soul.
- Release pain, anger, resentment, prejudices, judgment, criticism as well as fear of being hurt.
- See and live in the Creator's truth.
- Be one with everyone.
- Surrender and allow divine guidance.
- Be of service to others.
- Surround yourself with compassionate, kind and loving people and animals.
- See love as the answer.
- Know that it is possible for you to be compassionate towards everyone and that you deserve compassion.

Benefits: Letting go of anger and resentment towards yourself and others. Increase of love and compassion for yourself and others.

Affirmation: **"I am compassionate."**

Asana: Humble Warrior (Baddha Virabhadrasana)

From standing, step your right foot back and pivot your foot to about 1 o'clock. Bend your left knee, so your knee is above your ankle. Clasp your hands behind your back, roll your shoulders back and straighten your arms. Inhale, lengthen, and open your heart. Exhale, lean your torso forward with a straight back as you lift your hands away from your buttocks.

Lift your arms away from your back. Bring your torso to the inside of your left leg. Your left knee is still bent. As you are humbly bowing, take a few deep, slow breaths, mentally affirming **"I am compassionate".** Inhale your torso up slowly, release your arms, and step your right foot forward to meet the left.

Relax. Change sides, clasping your hands with the other thumb on top. **Enjoy the practice on this side.**

Benefits:

- Stretches the hip flexors, quadriceps, groin muscles, and legs.
- Counter-acts the effects of slouching and poor posture.
- Engages the core muscles, promoting stability and balance.
- Improves flexibility and range of motion in the spine and shoulders.
- Enhances focus, concentration, and mental resilience through the challenging balance component.
- Encourages introspection and humility, as the posture requires surrendering and bowing the head.
- Stimulates the abdominal organs, aiding digestion and detoxification.
- Builds self-confidence and perseverance.
- Cultivates a sense of gratitude and appreciation for the body's capabilities and limitations.

Asana: **Half Camel** (Ardha Ustrasana)

From your knees lift your buttocks off your heels, and place your hands on your hips. Inhale your left arm up, and exhale your right hand onto the earth on the outside of your right foot. If your hand does not reach the earth, just lean back, moving in that direction. Take a few deep, slow breaths, mentally affirming **"I am compassionate"**. Inhale your hands to your hips, and exhale to the starting position. Enjoy a few relaxing breaths here.

Change sides and enjoy the practice on this side.

Benefits:

- Stretches and opens the chest, shoulders, and heart center, promoting better posture and breathing.
- Improves spinal flexibility and mobility, especially in the thoracic spine.
- Engages and strengthens the muscles along the spine and in the back, promoting a healthy spine.
- Stimulates the abdominal organs, aiding digestion and promoting detoxification.
- Expands the ribcage and increases lung capacity, enhancing respiratory function.
- Relieves tension in the shoulders, neck, and upper back, reducing stiffness and discomfort.
- Opens the heart center and releases stored emotions, promoting a sense of emotional well-being.
- Encourages the flow of prana (life force energy) throughout the body, revitalizing the entire system.

Chair option

Sit on a chair with your back away from the back of the chair. Inhale your left arm up, bring your right hand to the lower right side of your chair back. Gently exhale and lean back. Take a few deep, slow breaths, mentally affirming **"I am compassionate"**. Inhale your arms up and spine to center. Exhale, relax your arms down. Enjoy a few relaxing breaths here. **Change sides, and enjoy the practice on this side.**

Asana: **Thread the needle** (Urdhva Mukha Pasasana)

On your hands and knees place your hands directly under your shoulders and knees under your hips. Inhale your right arm back and up. Exhale as you thread the needle, bringing your right arm under your torso and under your left arm with your palm up onto the earth. Rest your right cheek or ear onto the earth. Keep your hips raised. You can slide your left hand forward, extending the arm, or bring your left hand behind your lower back, towards your right hip. Adjust the pose to avoid straining your neck or shoulder. There is very little weight on your head. Allow every exhalation to gently open your shoulders and heart. Take several deep, slow breaths in this pose, mentally affirming **"I am compassionate"**. Place your left palm on the earth under your left shoulder, slide your right hand out and place your right palm under your right shoulder. **Change sides, and enjoy the practice on this side.**

Benefits:

- Stretches the shoulders, upper back, neck muscles, and improves posture.
- Relieves tension in the upper body.
- Releases tightness in the arms and shoulders.
- Stimulates the internal organs, aiding digestion and detoxification.
- Calms the mind and reduces stress.
- Improves flexibility and mobility in the spine.
- Can help alleviate symptoms of anxiety and fatigue.

Mudra: **Anjali Mudra: Open your heart with gratitude**

Place your palms at your heart chakra in prayer, mentally affirming **"I am compassionate"**. Focus on opening your heart and feeling compassion for yourself, other people, and animals.

Pranayama: **Three-part yogic breath** (Dirga Pranayama)

One of the most calming, grounding breathing exercises you can do. It really works to help focus your attention on the present moment and get in tune with the sensations of your physical body.

Place one hand on your heart and the other one on your belly. Breathe through the nose into your belly, push your belly out, draw the same breath up into your rib cage and chest, slowly exhale through the nose, then chest, ribs, and belly. Draw your belly in towards your spine.

Repeat for at least 10 cycles of breath.

Notice how centered and compassionate you feel.

Yoga for Courage

Living in fear does not serve anyone. It holds you back and restricts you physically, emotionally, mentally and in life. It is time for you to free yourself from fear, and step into courage!

Benefits: Healthy kidneys, liver, heart, and lungs. You will feel more courage, enthusiasm, and joy in your relationships and all areas of your life.

Affirmation: **"I am courageous!"**

Asana: **Lion** (Simhasana)

Sit with your hips on your heels and palms resting on your knees or legs. Inhale and reach the top of your head up to lengthen your spine. Arch your spine, look up at your third eye, your intuitive center between your eyebrows, stretch your tongue out and down and exhale through the mouth, roaring like a lion with a "haaa" sound. Inhale to the starting position and repeat three to five times, mentally affirming **"I am courageous!"**. **Notice how empowered and courageous you feel.**

Benefits:

- Relieves tension in the face, throat, and neck.
- Helps relieve fear and doubt.
- Helps reduce anxiety and improves mood.

Asana: **Bow** (Dhanurasana)

Lying on your belly with your legs hip distance apart, exhale while bending your knees. Lift your upper body up off the earth. Reach your right hand back and hold onto the outside of your right ankle. Reach your left hand back and hold onto the outside of your left ankle. You can just reach your arms back if it is challenging to touch your ankles. Gently lift your thighs away from the earth. Take five deep, slow breaths, mentally affirming **"I am courageous!"**. Let go of your ankles. Exhale, as you slowly roll onto your belly.

Benefits:

- Stretches the entire front of the body, including the abdomen, chest, and thighs.
- Strengthens the back muscles, including the erector spinae and rhomboids.
- Improves flexibility and mobility in the spine.
- Stimulates the digestive organs, aiding digestion and elimination.
- Opens up the shoulders and improves posture.
- Enhances lung capacity and respiratory function.
- Promotes balance and coordination.
- Releases tension and stress in the back and shoulders.
- Energizes the body and increases vitality.
- Can help alleviate mild back pain and discomfort.

Asana: **Goddess** (Utkata Konasana)

Stand with our feet wider than shoulder-width apart. Turn your feet slightly out, and bend your knees into a squat. Tuck your tailbone, and gently press your belly button in and up. Keep your knees over your ankles to protect your knees. Bring your arms into cactus pose, bending them at the elbows, palms facing forward with fingers extended up. Enjoy a few deep, slow breaths, mentally affirming **"I am courageous!"**. **Feel the strength, courage and empowerment** of the goddess within you. Step your right foot in and relax your arms down by your sides.

Benefits:

- Strengthens the legs, hips, and core muscles.
- Improves flexibility in the hips, groin, and inner thighs.
- Opens up the chest and shoulders, promoting better posture.
- Stimulates the abdominal organs, aiding digestion and elimination.
- Enhances balance and stability; cultivates focus and concentration.
- Relieves tension and stress in the hips and pelvic region.
- Empowers and energizes the yogi, fostering a sense of inner strength and confidence.

Mudra

Seated, bring your arms in a V position, palms facing up. Extend your thumbs, then curl in your other fingers and extend, repeat for about one minute, as you breathe calmly, mentally affirming **"I am courageous!"**

Pranayama: **Sitali breath**

This pranayama is physically and emotionally cooling. It is helpful in cooling our anxiety. It allows us to feel courageous from a calm state of being.

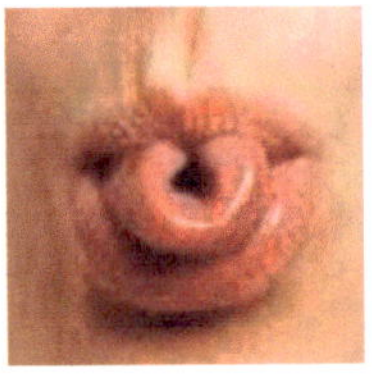

Stick your tongue out and curl the sides of tongue in like a tube. Breathe in through this tube, breathe out through your nose, repeat until fear and anxiety disappears, and your mind is calm.

Yoga for Hope

Positive change is possible for you now! No matter how much you have suffered, there is hope! Trust that you deserve to be healthy and happy, and you are worthy of it.

Benefits: Releasing tension in your back and shoulders and letting go of sadness and despair. Digesting food and life with ease and grace. Opening your heart and whole being to new possibilities and opportunities. Seeing light in all situations.

Affirmation: **"I have hope!"**

Asana: **Bridge** (Setu Bandha Sarvangasana)

Lie on your back, and bend your knees. Place your feet on the earth hip-width apart, close to your sit bones. Tuck your chin towards your chest. Inhale, as you slowly roll up your hips, lower back, and middle back. Interlace your hands behind your back with your arms straight. Keep lifting your hips as you take a few deep, slow breaths, mentally affirming **"I have hope!"**

This bridge of hope is helping you to **move from pain to peace.**

Release your hands. Exhale, and slowly roll down, one vertebra at a time. You may like to draw your knees towards your chest for a few breaths, then extend them onto the earth.

Benefits:

- Strengthens the back, glutes, and legs while also stretching the chest and spine.
- It can help alleviate back pain.
- Improves balance and stability.
- Reduces anxiety and depression.
- Increases spinal flexibility

Asana: **Airplane** (Dekasana)

From standing, extend your arms out to either side. Slowly lean forward, and extend your right leg back. Take a few deep, slow breaths in this pose, mentally affirming **"I have hope!"** Fly into new, unlimited possibilities! Exhale your leg down. **Change legs.**

Benefits:

- Strengthens the legs and the muscles along the spine, promoting spinal health and alignment.
- Engages the core muscles, including the abdominals and obliques, to stabilize the body.
- Opens up the chest and shoulders, promoting better posture.
- Stretches the arms and back, enhancing flexibility and mobility in the upper body.
- Stimulates circulation throughout the body, invigorating the cardiovascular system.
- Increases focus, concentration and improves balance of body and mind.
- Builds confidence and mental resilience.
- Provides a sense of expansion and freedom in the body, fostering a feeling of lightness and vitality.

Floor option: You can practice this pose lying on your belly. Inhale your head and chest up, extend your arms out to either side and up, and lift your straight legs up off the earth.

Take a few deep, slow breaths in this pose, mentally affirming **"I have hope!"** Fly into new, unlimited possibilities! Exhale, slowly lower onto your belly.

Asana: **Deep belly twist** (Jathara Parivartanasana)

Seated, straighten your left leg out in front of you on the earth. Place the sole of your right foot against your inner left thigh. Place your left hand on your right knee and right hand in the right back corner of your mat. Inhale, lengthen your spine, exhale, draw the belly in towards the spine, and lean over your right knee. Feel free to round your back over your knee. This is not a spinal twist, but a deep belly twist. Take a few deep, slow breaths in this pose, mentally affirming **"I have hope!"** on the inhalation, exhale and twist, while breathing out everything that is preventing you from feeling hope. Let go of physical and emotional indigestion, so you will feel clear to experience hope. Inhale as you raise your arms above your head, straighten your right leg in front of you. Exhale as you lower your palms to your heart. **Change sides, and enjoy this pose on this side.**

Benefits:

- Stretches and releases tension in the muscles of the back, spine, and hips.
- Improves spinal mobility and flexibility, particularly in the thoracic and lumbar regions, which helps to improve posture.
- Massages the abdominal organs, aiding in digestion and detoxification.
- Relieves lower back pain and discomfort.
- Stimulates the nervous system, promoting relaxation and stress relief.
- Encourages deep breathing and diaphragmatic engagement, promoting relaxation and calmness.
- Can alleviate discomfort associated with menstrual cramps and digestive issues.
- Cultivates a sense of internal awareness and introspection, fostering a peaceful connection between mind and body.

Mudra: **Highest Enlightenment** (Uttarabodhi) **Mudra**

Seated, place both hands clasped in front of your solar plexus, at your stomach. Place your index fingers together and thumbs together, extending them. Rotate your hands inward, so your index fingers point up to the sky and thumbs down to the earth at the stomach level. Hold for as long as you like, mentally affirming **"I have hope!".** Repeat whenever you need hope and inspiration.

Pranayama: **Breath of Fire** (Kapalabhati)

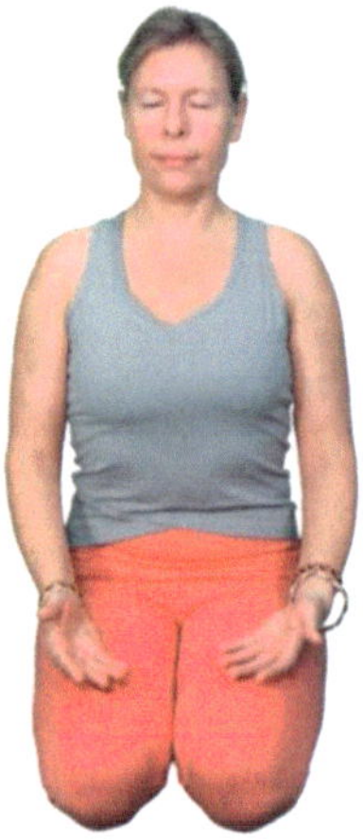

The breath of fire helps us to activate the digestive fire, to purify our body, thoughts and emotions and clear the path, so we can digest life with ease, grace and joy.

Close your eyes, and gently lift your gaze to your third eye, your intuitive center between your eyebrows. Inhale through the nose, exhale sharply through the nose while pulling in the belly towards the spine. The inhalation happens naturally, the sharp exhalation is the focus. Breathe out despair, frustration, pain or whatever you like to release. Breathe in hope. Repeat at least 20 times. If you get light headed, open your eyes, and return to your regular breath.

Yoga for Inner Wisdom

You can read hundreds of books and acquire a lot of knowledge, but true wisdom is when you integrate that knowledge into your own being in your unique way. When you become one with it, you experience it on a deep level, and express that inner wisdom through your feelings, thoughts, and actions. You need to go within to cultivate true inner wisdom.

Benefits: Clarity, confidence, and peace. These beautiful soul qualities are exactly what the world needs! Through your embodiment and expression of them, you will be able to bring more value to the world.

Affirmation: **"I trust my inner wisdom."**

Asana: **Triangle** (Trikonasana)

From standing, step your left foot out to the left and turn your foot out. Turn to face that direction. Inhale as you lift your arms out to the sides, on the exhalation hinge and lean your torso over your left leg. Keep your spine straight as you bring your left hand down alongside your leg and right arm up. The left hand may touch the earth on the inside of your left foot. It is more important to keep your spine straight than to place your hand on the earth. It is fine if your hand touches your inner thigh, knee or calf. Take a few deep, slow breaths in this pose, mentally affirming **"I trust my inner wisdom"**.

In this symbol of the Divine you are reaching for the heavens while being connected to the earth. Inhale as you bring your arms out to the sides, pivot your left foot forward. **Change sides, and enjoy this pose on this side.**

Asana: **Eagle** (Garudasana)

From Mountain Pose, standing with both feet next to each other, arms alongside your body, inhale your arms up above your head. Exhale your right elbow under your left. Your palms may touch or move towards each other. Maintaining this pose, inhale your arms up to feel a stretch in your shoulders. Take a few breaths, mentally affirming **"I trust my inner wisdom"**.

Exhale your elbows down. Bend your knees, wrap your right knee over the left knee. Your toes can touch the ground on the outside of your left foot or you can wrap your right foot around your left ankle. Squeeze under your ankles, ground, armpits, elbow and wrists to activate the lymphatic system. Take a few breaths, silently repeating your affirmation. Relax your arms and legs and return to Mountain Pose. Enjoy a few breaths here. **Change sides, and enjoy this pose on this side.**

Benefits:

- Stretches the shoulders, upper back, and outer thighs, and relieves tension.
- Strengthens the muscles of the legs, including the quadriceps and calves.
- Opens the hips and increases hip mobility.
- Activates lymphatic system.
- Engages the core muscles, promoting stability and balance.
- Enhances focus, concentration, relaxation and stress relief.
- Increases circulation to the arms and legs, promoting overall circulation and vitality.
- Cultivates a sense of mental and physical resilience.
- Can help reduce pain and disability in people with chronic low back pain.

Asana: **Pigeon** (Kapotasana)

If you have knee pain, you may prefer practicing the Supine Figure Four Option below. Feel it out for your own body.

For Pigeon start in Downward Facing Dog. From here bring your right knee behind your right hand. Angle your shin under your torso and bring your right foot to the left. Slide your left foot back, uncurl your toes. Feel free to place a folded blanket under our right buttocks for support. Adjust your knee, so you do not feel tension in your knee. Come onto your fingertips, roll your shoulders back to open your heart and lengthen your spine. Exhale as you lower your torso and rest your head on your hands or reach your arms forward on the earth and rest your forehead on the earth.

You could also rest your arms alongside your body, palms facing up.

Take a few deep, slow breaths, mentally affirming **"I trust my inner wisdom"**. Slide your palms on the earth underneath your shoulders. Press into your palms, lift your torso, curl the toes of your left foot, lift your left knee off the earth, and exhale while stepping your right foot back into downward facing dog, **Change sides, and enjoy this pose on this side.**

Benefits:

- Stretches the hips, glutes, and hip rotator muscles.
- Increases hip flexibility and range of motion.
- Relieves tension and tightness in the hip area.
- Helps alleviate symptoms of sciatica and lower back pain.
- Promotes relaxation and releases stored emotions.

Asana: **Supine Figure Four Option** (Sucirandhrasana)

Lie on your back. Bend your knees with your heels close to your sit bones. Cross the right ankle over the left knee. Lift your left foot off the earth. Reach your right hand through between your thighs. and clasp your hands a couple of inches below your left knee or behind your thigh. Your right elbow can press your leg away from you to deepen the stretch in your hip. Take a few deep, slow breaths, mentally affirming **"I trust my inner wisdom"**. Relax your arms by your sides, and place your feet on the earth. **Change sides, and enjoy this pose on this side.**

Benefits:

- Stretches and increases flexibility in the hips, particularly the piriformis and glute muscles.

- Alleviates tension and discomfort in the lower back by releasing tightness in the hip muscles.
- Enhances range of motion in the hip joint, promoting better mobility and ease of movement.
- Helps relieve sciatic pain by releasing tension on the sciatic nerve that may be caused by tight hip muscles.
- Can be used as a post-workout stretch to relax and rejuvenate the muscles after physical activity.
- Encourages a sense of relaxation and calmness by releasing tension in the hips and lower back.
- Enhances blood circulation to the hip and gluteal muscles, supporting their recovery and overall health.
- Promotes mindfulness and body awareness as you focus on the sensations in your hips and lower back during the stretch.

Mudra: **Mudra of the Inner Self**

Place the base of your hands, thumbs and finger tips together at your heart chakra. Mentally affirm **"I trust my inner wisdom"**. Feel the gentle, yet strong assurance in your heart.

Pranayama: **Measured Breathing** (Sama Vritti)

This practice creates balance in our brain and heart, which helps us to tune into and trust our intuition.

Inhale through the nose for a count of 4 or 5 (deep and slow, but not stressful), hold the breath for the same count, exhale through the nose for the same count. Keep the breath out for the same count.

Repeat at least 10 times. Notice how calm and clear you are.

Trust your inner wisdom!

Yoga for Joy

Whether your current way of life just feels mundane, or you are experiencing deep frustration or pain. This is a great time to open up to more joy!

Benefits: Release of pain and tension, lightness of being, enhanced relationships and quality of life. When you feel joy within you, you will naturally attract joyful people and situations.

Affirmation: **"I am joy!"**

Asana: **Reclined Butterfly** (Supta Baddha Konasana)

Lie on your back with the soles of your feet touching and knees out to the sides. Feel free to place folded blankets under your knees for support. Bring your arms in a relaxed position along your sides. As an option, you can bring them into the cactus position by bending 90 degrees at your elbows. Allow your cactus arms and backs of hands to touch the earth or move towards the earth.

Enjoy a few deep, slow breaths in this open surrender pose, mentally affirming **"I am joy!"**.

Benefits:

- Opens the hips and stretches the inner thighs and groin muscles.
- Provides a gentle stretch for the spine, promoting flexibility and mobility.
- Relieves tension and stiffness in the lower back and pelvic area.
- Promotes relaxation. reduces stress and promotes a sense of inner peace and tranquility.
- Stimulates the abdominal organs, aiding digestion and elimination.
- Improves blood circulation to the pelvic region, which can be beneficial for reproductive health and to alleviate symptoms of menstrual discomfort and menopausal symptoms.

Asana: **Modified Wild Thing** (Ardha Camatkarasana)

Sit with your right leg out straight and left leg bent. Press the sole of your left foot against your inner right thigh. Place your left hand behind you on the earth. As you inhale, lift your hips and chest, and extend your right arm alongside your ear. Enjoy a few deep, slow breaths in this heart opener, mentally affirming **"I am joy!"**. Exhale, as you lower your arm and hips. **Change sides, and enjoy the practice on this side.**

Benefits:

- Opens the chest and shoulders, stretching the front of the body.
- Strengthens the arms, shoulders, and upper back.
- Stretches and lengthens the spine, improving flexibility and mobility.
- Engages the core muscles, promoting stability and balance.
- Stimulates the cardiovascular system and increases heart rate, providing a mild cardiovascular workout.
- Enhances mood and mental well-being by releasing endorphins and reducing stress.
- Improves coordination.
- Encourages a sense of playfulness and freedom in movement; can be empowering and confidence-building as it challenges balance and strength in a dynamic way.
- Offers a gentle inversion, promoting blood flow to the brain and energizing the body.

Asana: **Fish** (Matsyasana)

Lie on your back with your arms by your sides, close to your torso. Lift your pelvis slightly off the earth, and slide your hands, palms facing down, underneath your buttocks. Inhale and press into forearms and elbows. Bring your shoulder blades towards each other. Arch your spine, lift your chest, and place your crown (top of the head)

gently on the earth with very little weight on it. Do not move your head to the sides to avoid creating tension in your neck. Enjoy a few deep, slow breaths in this heart opening pose, mentally affirming **"I am joy!"**. Tuck your chin towards your chest, release your arms and hands to your sides, and slowly roll down.

Benefits:

- Stretches the chest, throat, and abdomen.
- Opens the shoulders and improves posture.
- Relieves tension and fatigue in the upper back and neck.
- Enhances lung capacity and improves breathing.
- Promotes relaxation and helps alleviate stress and anxiety.

Mudra: **Prana (Life Force) Mudra**

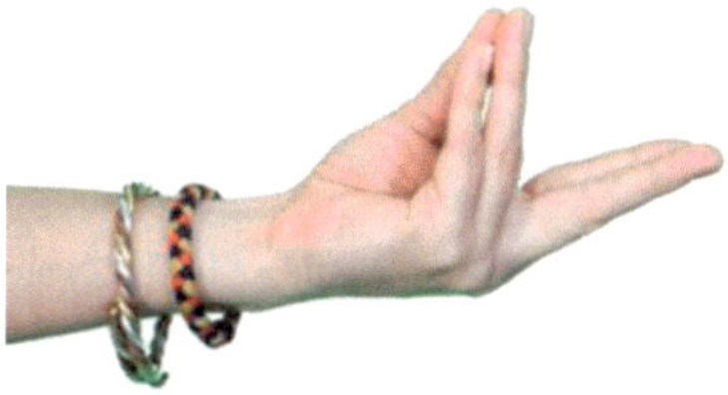

Like a closed-up peace sign, this simple gesture harnesses the positive flow of life-force energy and increases vitality and enthusiasm for life. If you feel fatigued or worn out, this mudra can give you a natural boost of energy.

Bring the tips of the ring and little fingers together with the thumb. Extend your index and middle fingers. Hold your hands in Prana Mudra while taking several deep breaths, mentally affirming **"I am joy!".**

Notice how joyful you feel.

Pranayama: **Breath of Joy** (Ananda Pranayama)

Standing, inhale arms forward, inhale arms out to the sides, inhale arms up (as if you are sipping in small breaths through the nose), exhale through the mouth, your arms down into a forward bend.

Repeat at least 10 times, mentally affirming **"I am joy!"** Feel the joy within you!

Yoga for Loving Kindness

Non-harming or loving kindness is the first limb of yoga. Are you as loving and kind to yourself as you are to others? Are you holding on to judgments about yourself or others? Is it challenging for you to forgive? Anger, criticism, and holding onto grudges only creates more frustration and anger in and around us. Everyone wants to feel accepted and loved. Embrace loving kindness and share it with the world!

Benefits: Release of tension, judgment, resentment and anger. Balancing of your nervous system, right and left hemispheres of your brain, softening of your energy, and surrender. Your loving kindness will help others to feel safe and loved and uplift you as well as everyone around you.

Affirmation: "I am loving and kind."

Asana: Bridge (Setu Bandha Sarvangasana)

Lie on your back, and bend your knees. Place your feet on the earth hip-width apart, close to your sit bones. Tuck your chin towards your chest. Inhale, as you slowly roll up your hips, lower back, and middle back. Interlace your hands behind your back with your arms straight. Keep lifting your hips as you take a few deep, slow breaths, mentally affirming **"I am loving and kind"**.

Release your hands. Exhale, and slowly roll down, one vertebrae at a time. You may like to draw your knees towards your chest for a few breaths, then extend them onto the earth.

Benefits:

- Strengthens the back, glutes, and legs while also stretching the chest and spine.
- It can help alleviate back pain.
- Improves balance and stability.
- Reduces anxiety and depression.
- Increases spinal flexibility.

Asana: **Humble Warrior** (Baddha Virabhadrasana)

From standing, step your right foot back and pivot your foot to about 1 o'clock. Bend your left knee, so your knee is above your ankle. Clasp your hands behind your back, roll your shoulders back and straighten your arms. Inhale, lengthen, and open your heart. Exhale, lean your torso forward with a straight back as you lift your hands away from your buttocks. Lift your arms away from your back. Bring your torso to the inside of your left leg. Your left knee is still bent. As you are humbly bowing, take a few deep, slow breaths, mentally affirming **"I am loving and kind"**.

Inhale, as you lift up your torso slowly, exhale, as you release your arms, and step your right foot forward to meet the left. Relax.

Change sides, clasping your hands with the other thumb on top. Enjoy the practice on this side.

Benefits:

- Stretches the hip flexors, quadriceps, groin muscles, and legs.
- Counter-acts the effects of slouching and poor posture.
- Engages the core muscles, promoting stability and balance.
- Improves flexibility and range of motion in the spine and shoulders.
- Enhances focus, concentration, and mental resilience through the challenging balance component.
- Encourages introspection and humility, as the posture requires surrendering and bowing the head.
- Stimulates the abdominal organs, aiding digestion and detoxification.
- Builds self-confidence and perseverance.
- Cultivates a sense of gratitude and appreciation for the body's capabilities and limitations.

Asana: **Legs Up The Wall** (Viparita Karani)

Lie on your back, facing a wall with knees bent. Your buttocks are close to the wall. Extend your legs up against the wall, and enjoy a few deep, slow breaths in this inversion. mentally affirming **"I am loving and kind"**. Blood and oxygen are flowing to your heart, energizing it with loving kindness.

Exhale, as you bend your knees towards your chest. Slowly roll onto your right side, and either extend your legs on the earth or gently press up into a seated position.

Benefits:

- Promotes relaxation and relieves stress, promoting mental clarity and emotional balance.
- Improves circulation by allowing blood to flow more easily from the feet and legs back to the heart.
- Reduces swelling in the lower extremities by facilitating lymphatic drainage.
- Alleviates tension in the legs, lower back, and hips, and increases flexibility and mobility.
- Helps to relieve mild back pain and discomfort.
- May help to alleviate symptoms of mild anxiety and depression.
- Can be practiced as a restorative pose to rejuvenate the body and mind after a long day or intense physical activity and to help alleviate insomnia.

Mudra: **Lotus** (Padma) **Mudra -** Rising from muddy waters into purity.

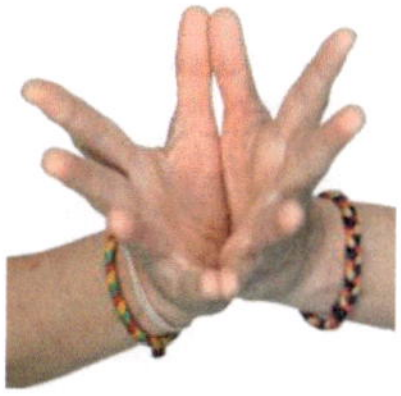

With your palms at your heart, touch the outer edges of both pinky fingers and thumbs together. Keep the heels of the palms pressed together as you blossom open through your hands. Extend through the tips of all 10 fingers. Mentally affirm **"I am loving and kind"**.

Pranayama: **Alternate Nostril Breathing** (Nadi Shodhana)

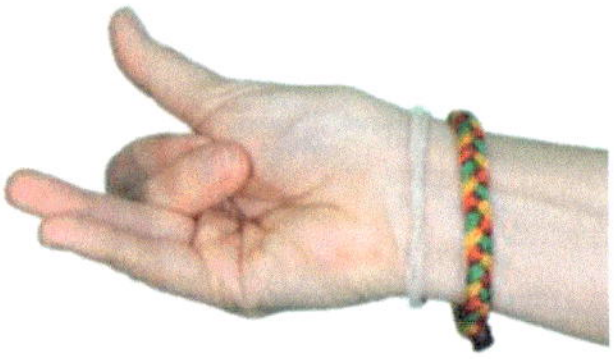

Place your right hand close to your nose. Tuck your index and middle fingers in. Inhale through both nostrils. Close your right nostril with your thumb, keeping index and middle fingers tucked in.

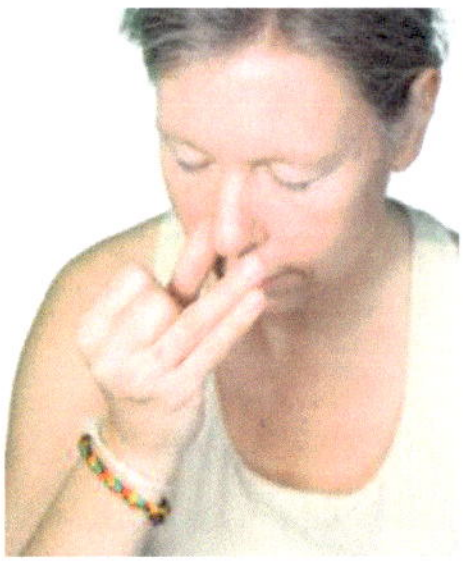

Exhale through your left nostril. Keep the breath out for a few seconds.

Inhale through your left nostril, close the left with your ring and little fingers.

Exhale through the right nostril. Keep the breath out for a few seconds.

Inhale through the right, exhale through the left.

Continue this flow for about five minutes, always changing sides after the inhalation. If you feel lightheaded at any point, return to your regular breath.

Notice how calm, loving and kind you feel.

Yoga for Oneness

You are always one with all that is. Sometimes you may feel separate, and this can create a feeling of insecurity, loneliness, and confusion. Feeling separate can also cause illness over time. You are not separate. You are one with the Creator!

Benefits: Letting go of doubt, the sense of separation, loneliness, and illness. Strengthening of life force within you, and establishment of the trust that you and God are one. That you are never alone. And that you are guided in the right direction.

Affirmation: **"I am One with All That is"**

Asana: **Sphinx** (Salamba Bhujangasana)

Lie on your belly. Place your elbows directly underneath your shoulder blades. Press the tops of your feet into the earth, and engage your quadriceps. Inhale, as you lift your upper body, leading with your heart. Exhale, draw the earth towards you with your hands. Repeat this subtle lengthening and drawing the earth towards you, as you mentally affirm **"I am one with all that is"**. Feel your connection with the earth and sky, and with universal life force.

Exhale, as you slowly lower your upper body onto your belly. Relax your arms by your sides.

Benefits:

- Stretches the chest, abdomen, and spine.
- Opens the front of the body, improving posture.
- Strengthens the back muscles, supporting the spine.
- Helps relieve mild back pain and discomfort.
- Promotes relaxation and stress relief.

Asana: **Five-Pointed Star** (Utthita Tadasana)

From standing, step your feet wide apart with your arms extended out to the sides, palms facing down. Tuck your tailbone, engage your legs, and feel that you are rooted into the earth. Lengthen your crown up. Reach out through your fingertips and relax your shoulders down and back. As you extend out to five directions, take a few deep, slow breaths, and mentally affirm **"I am one with all that is"**. Step your feet to hip width, and exhale, as you lower your arms.

Benefits:

- Strengthens the legs, ankles, and feet.
- Improves balance and stability.
- Stretches the inner thighs and groin.
- Promotes good posture and body alignment.
- Increases body awareness and mindfulness.

Asana: **Extended Side-Angle** (Utthita Parsvakonasana)

From standing, step your left foot back, and pivot your left foot to about 11 o'clock. Bend your right knee, so it is directly above your ankle. Exhale, as you extend your torso over your right leg, and lower your right arm down. Your forearm can rest on your thigh, or extend straight down along the inside or outside of your right leg. Inhale, as you extend your left arm over your head alongside your ear. Extend from the outside of your left heel through your fingertips, and turn your rib cage towards the sky. You can look up if this does not create tension in your neck. Allow the exhalation to gently deepen the pose, as you bend your right knee a little more deeply. Your knee is still above your ankle. Enjoy a few deep, slow breaths, mentally affirming **"I am one with all that is"**. Inhale, as you lift your torso and left arm up. Exhale, step your left foot forward to meet the right. **Change sides, and enjoy this practice on this side.**

Benefits:

- Stretches and strengthens the legs, hips, and waist.
- Opens the chest and shoulders.
- Increases flexibility and range of motion in the spine.
- Builds lower body strength and stability.
- Enhances balance and body awareness.

Chair option: Bring your left leg out to the left, and straighten your left leg. Bring your right foot to the right, with your knee bent above your ankle. Place your right forearm on your right leg. As you inhale, extend your left arm up alongside your ear. Enjoy a few deep, slow breaths, mentally affirming **"I am one with all that is"**. Inhale, as you lift your torso and left arm up. Exhale, bring your feet to center. Change sides, and enjoy this practice on this side.

Mudra: Chin (Consciousness) Mudra

Place your thumb and index finger together on each hand. Extend the other fingers. Rest your hands on your thighs with palms facing down.

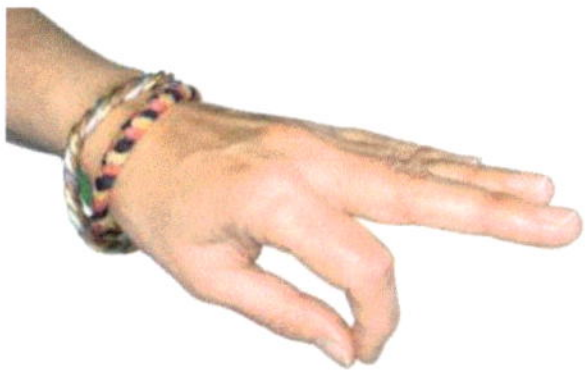

Focus on your individualized soul uniting with the supreme soul. Enjoy the following pranayama with eyes closed and your gaze gently lifted to your third eye between your eyebrows.

Pranayama: **Measured breathing** (Sama Vritti)

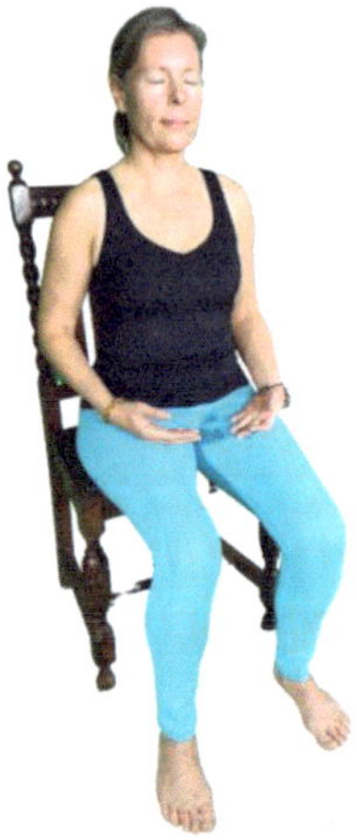

Breathe through your nose, inhale for a count of 5 or 6. Hold your breath for the same count. Exhale through the nose for the same count. Keep the breath out for the same count.

Continue for at least 10 cycles of breath. Feel one with your body, mind, soul, and the Creator of all that is.

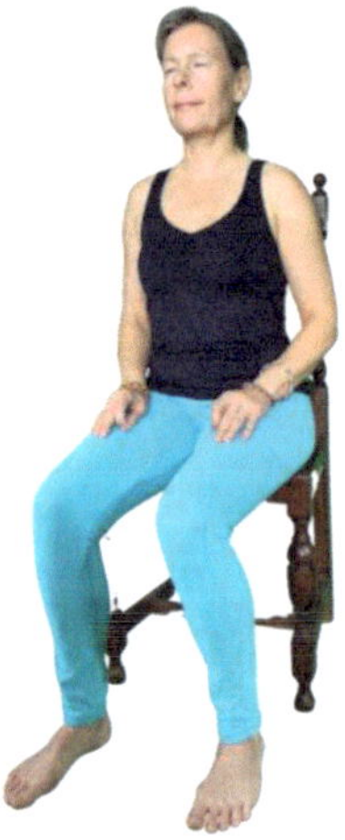

Yoga for Peace

World peace starts with you! When you feel peace, you naturally shine it out into the world, without needing to do anything. Restlessness, worry, sadness, fear, and anger prevents you from feeling deep peace.

Benefits: Letting go of restlessness, worry, and other limiting emotions. A soothing feeling of calm, centeredness, and relaxation. Being at peace with your whole being and all situations you are experiencing.

Affirmation: "I am peace."

Asana: Tree (Vrkasana)

Stand with both feet firmly rooted into the earth. Look at one spot in front of you that does not move. Place your right foot against your inner left calf or thigh. Your toes can also touch the ground for more stability. Your arms can be out to the sides, or you can place your palms at your heart center in Anjali Mudra. If you feel stable, allow your breath to reach your arms up. Ground into the earth and reach up to the heavens. Take a few deep, mindful breaths, while mentally affirming **"I am peace"**. Exhale, as you lower your arms and foot.

Change sides and enjoy this practice on this side.

Benefits:

- Improves balance and reduces falls.
- Reduces stress and anxiety.
- Improves joint position sense.
- Increases muscle strength, endurance and balance.

Supine Option: You can practice Tree on your back, following the same instructions as above.

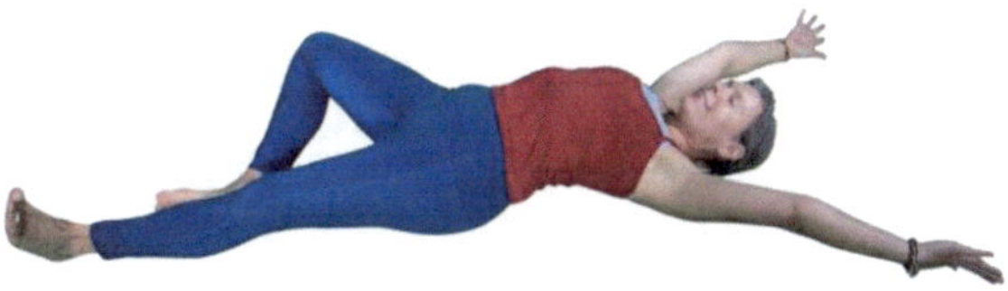

Asana: **Half Splits** (Ardha Hanumanasana)

Begin in a low lunge with your right foot forward, and left knee resting on the earth. Feel free to place a folded blanket or towel under your knee. Your left knee is underneath your hips. Place your fingertips on the earth on either side of your front foot.

Move your hands back underneath your shoulders, as you extend your right leg forward. Place your right heel on the earth, and flex your right foot. Your left hip and knee are still stacked. Exhale, as you fold your torso forward. Enjoy a few deep, slow breaths, while mentally affirming **"I am peace"**. Inhale, as you lift your torso. Exhale into a low lunge.

Change sides and enjoy this practice on this side.

Benefits:

- Stretches the hamstrings and calf muscles, increasing flexibility in the back of the legs.
- Improves hip flexibility and mobility by targeting the hip flexors.
- Relieves tension in the lower back and hips, lengthens the spine and helps to improve posture.
- Strengthens the legs.
- Can help alleviate sciatica pain by stretching the sciatic nerve.
- Stimulates circulation in the lower body, promoting blood flow to the legs and feet.
- Provides a mild inversion effect, which can help to calm the mind and reduce stress.
- Enhances balance and concentration.

Asana: **Happy Baby** (Ananda Balasana)

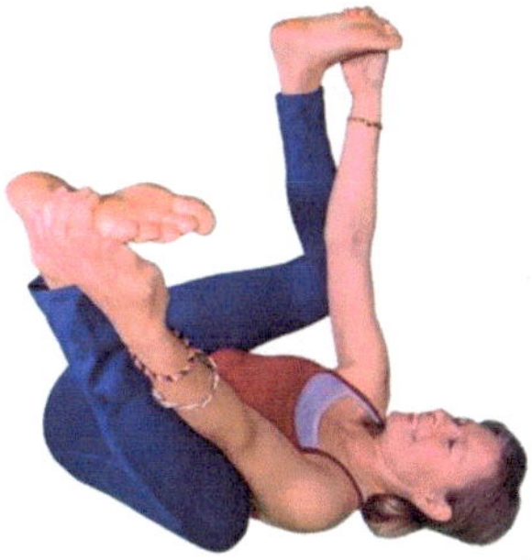

Lying on your back, bend your knees towards your chest with your soles facing up towards the sky. Hold on to the soles of your feet, and relax your knees out to the sides. Your spine is supported by the earth. Gently rock from side to side, or enjoy stillness. Take a few deep, slow breaths, while mentally affirming **"I am peace"**.

If you like you could release one foot onto the earth and rock from side to side, while mentally affirming **"I am peace"**.

Benefits:

- Stretches the inner thighs, groin, and hamstrings, promoting flexibility in the lower body.
- Relieves tension in the lower back and spine.
- Opens the hips and pelvis, improving mobility and range of motion.
- Stimulates the digestive organs, aiding in digestion and relieving bloating.
- Releases tension and stress from the body, promoting relaxation, a sense of calm, grounding, connection with the earth, childlike playfulness and joy.
- Helps to alleviate discomfort associated with menstrual cramps.

Mudra: **Angeli (Prayer) Mudra**

Place your palms together at your heart, fingers pointed up. Mentally affirm **"I am peace"**.

Pranayama: **Swooning Breath** (Murcha Pranayama)

Inhale through your nose as you slowly tilt your head back, and hold the breath for a few seconds.

Exhale through the nose as you slowly lower your chin towards your chest, keep the breath out for a few seconds.

Repeat for at least 10 cycles of breath.

Now relax your head in a neutral position, and feel deep peace.

Yoga for Truth

You may have strong opinions about what you and others should do or not do, but they are not necessarily based on Truth. Everyone is expressing their reality based on their individual truth as they know it. Let's align your truth with Universal Truth! YOUR authentic Truth!

Benefits: Letting go of judgment and attachments. Opening to a higher Truth that is in alignment with your soul and purpose. A feeling of connection, deep knowing, acceptance, and peace

Affirmation: "I am one with Universal Truth."

Asana: Reclined butterfly (Supta Baddha Konasana)

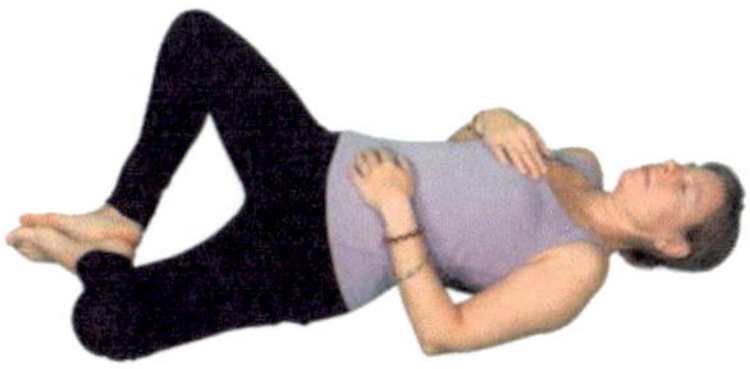

Lie on your back, souls of the feet touching with your knees out to the sides. Place one hand on your chest, the other hand on the belly.

Notice where you are holding on to tension and relax. Take a few deep, slow breaths, mentally affirming **"I am one with Universal Truth"**.

With each breath you are cultivating truth in your solar plexus, your power center, heart chakra and whole being.

Benefits:

- Opens the hips and stretches the inner thighs and groin muscles.
- Provides a gentle stretch for the spine, promoting flexibility and mobility.
- Relieves tension and stiffness in the lower back and pelvic area.
- Reduces stress, promotes relaxation, inner peace and tranquility.
- Stimulates the abdominal organs, aiding digestion and elimination.
- Improves blood circulation to the pelvic region, which can be beneficial for reproductive health and to alleviate symptoms of menstrual discomfort and menopausal symptoms.

Asana: **Triangle** (Trikonasana)

From standing, step your left foot out to the left and turn your foot out. Turn to face that direction. Inhale as you lift your arms out to the sides, on the exhalation hinge and lean your torso over your left leg.

Keep your spine straight as you bring your left hand down alongside your leg and right arm up. The left hand may touch the earth on the inside of your left foot.

It is more important to keep your spine straight than to place your hand on the earth. It is fine if your hand touches your inner thigh, knee or calf. Take a few deep, slow breaths in this pose, mentally affirming **"I am one with Universal Truth"**.

In this symbol of the Divine you are reaching for the heavens while being connected to the earth. Inhale as you bring your arms out to the sides, pivot your left foot forward.

Change sides, and enjoy this practice on this side.

Benefits:

- Stretches the hips, hamstrings, and spine.
- Strengthens the legs, knees, and ankles.
- It can also help improve digestion.
- Reduces neck pain.
- Improves balance and stability.
- Reduces stress and anxiety.
- Increases hip flexibility.

Asana: **Forward Bend with Twist** (Parivrtta Uttanasana)

From standing, place your hands on your hips, and exhale your torso into a forward bend. Release your hands onto the earth or shins. Place your right hand in front of your right toes, bend your right knee, engage your belly, and inhale your left arm up. Stay here or wrap your left arm around your back, touching the right hip crease.

Take a few deep, slow breaths in this pose, mentally affirming **"I am one with Universal Truth"**.

Unwrap your arm, return to a forward bend, and change sides. **Enjoy this practice on this side.**

Benefits:

- Stretches the hamstrings, lower back, and spine, promoting flexibility and releasing tension.
- Opens the chest and shoulders, enhancing mobility and improving posture.
- Massages the abdominal organs, aiding in digestion and promoting detoxification as well as helping alleviate menstrual discomfort.
- Stimulates the nervous system, promoting relaxation, mental clarity, and reducing stress and anxiety.
- Enhances spinal alignment and symmetry, reducing the risk of imbalances or injuries.
- Can help alleviate lower back pain and discomfort by gently stretching and releasing tight muscles.

Mudra: **Truth (Tattva) Mudra**:

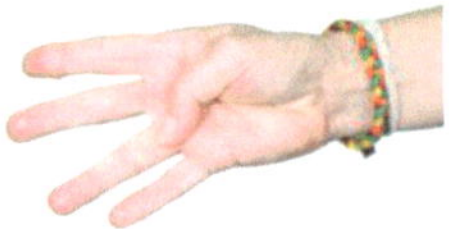

Place your thumbs onto the base of your ring fingers (each hand) and extend your other fingers out.

Rest your hands, palms facing up, on your thighs, and connect with the universal truth within you.

Pranayama: **Alternate Nostril Breathing** (Nadi Shodhana)

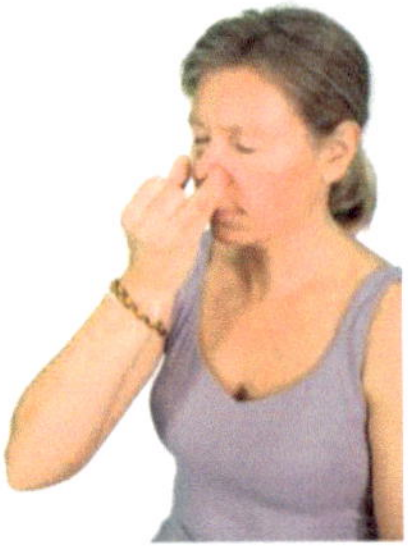

Balances the left and right hemispheres of the brain, as well as masculine and feminine energies in the body. It is a deeply purifying and balancing form of pranayama that promotes relaxation and reduces stress and anxiety. When you feel calm, you can tap into Universal Truth.

Place your right hand close to your nose. Tuck your index and middle fingers in. Inhale through both nostrils. Close your right nostril with your thumb, keeping index and middle fingers tucked in.

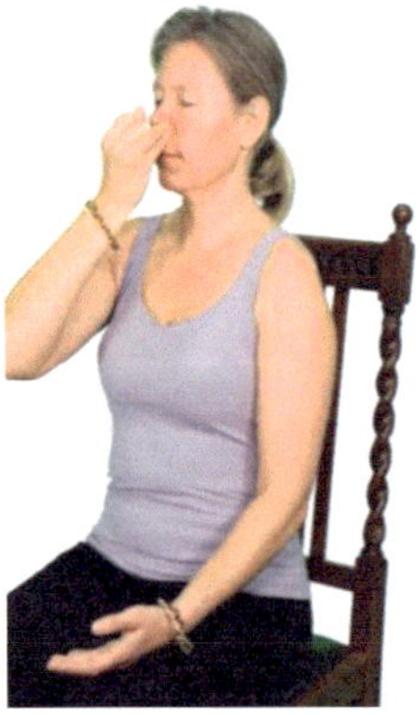

Exhale through your left nostril. Keep the breath out for a few seconds. Inhale through your left nostril, close the left with your ring and little fingers.

Exhale through the right nostril. Keep the breath out for a few seconds. Inhale through the right, exhale through the left.

Continue this flow for about five minutes, always changing sides after the inhalation. If you feel lightheaded at any point, return to your regular breath.

Notice how clear and connected you feel with Universal Truth.

Yoga for Chakra Balancing

When your chakras are open and balanced, prana (life force) flows through your spine gracefully. This practice will open and balance your seven chakras (energy centers) along the spine. This will help you to feel centered, receptive, open and balanced.

Benefits: Release of stress and tension, feeling connected, centered, open, receptive, and peaceful. These positive qualities will enhance your health, reduce inflammation, pain, and help you to flow through your life with divine guidance, ease, and grace.

Affirmation for the whole chakra practice: "I am open and balanced."

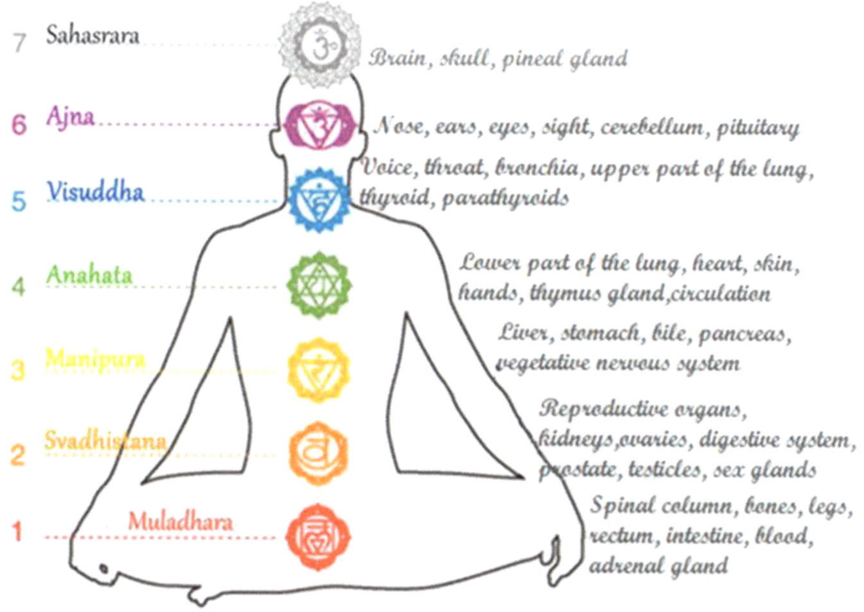

1st chakra: Muladhara (Root)

Element: **Earth**

Chant: **Lam**

Affirmation: **"I am grounded and connected to the earth."**

Asana: **Chair pose** (Utkatasana)

From standing, bend your knees, shift your weight into your heels, and inhale your arms up. If you feel pain in your shoulders, bring your arms forward.

Take at least five deep, slow breaths, mentally affirming **"I am grounded and connected to the earth"**.

Feel that you are rooted into the earth and supported by the earth.

Inhale as you straighten your legs . Exhale as you relax your arms down by your side.

Benefits:

- Strengthens the legs and glutes, enhancing lower body strength and stability.
- Improves core stability and posture by engaging the abdominal muscles to maintain balance.
- Stretches the shoulders, chest, and spine, promoting flexibility and relieving tension in the upper body.
- Stimulates circulation and blood flow throughout the body, providing a mild cardiovascular workout.
- Builds endurance and concentration, especially when holding the pose for an extended period.
- Provides a gentle stretch to the ankles and Achilles tendons, which can help alleviate stiffness and discomfort.

Seated (chair) option: Sit on a chair with your feet firmly on the earth. Inhale your arms up above your head. If you feel pain in your shoulders, bring your arms forward. Take at least five deep, slow breaths, mentally affirming **"I am grounded and connected to the earth"**. Feel that you are rooted into the earth and supported by the earth. Exhale as you relax your arms down by your sides.

Asana: **Warrior 1** (Virabhadrasana I)

From standing, step your left foot back, pivot your left foot to about 11 o'clock. Bend your right knee, so it is above your ankle. This protects your knee. Inhale your arms up above your head. Slightly bring your left hip forward and right hip back.

Enjoy deep, slow breaths, mentally affirming **"I am grounded and connected to the earth"**. Feel your strength in your connection with the earth.

Change sides and enjoy this pose on this side.

Benefits:

- Strengthens the legs, ankles, back, chest and lungs.
- Can help improve concentration, determination and focus.
- Improves shoulder range of motion.
- Reduces neck pain, stress, and anxiety.
- Increases leg strength and balance.

Chair option: Sit on a chair with the chair back on your right side. Hold on to the chair back with your right hand. Your right knee is directly underneath your hip. Keep your right hip on the chair, and slide your left foot back. Slightly bring your left hip forward and right hip back. If you like, you can inhale, as you raise your left arm, and take a few deep, slow breaths here. If you feel stable, pressing the toes and ball of your back foot into the earth, you could raise both arms, and take a few deep, slow breaths here. Mentally affirm **"I am grounded and connected to the earth"**.

Change sides and enjoy this pose on this side.

Asana: **Warrior 2** (Virabhadrasana II)

From standing, step your left foot back, pivot your left foot to about 11 o'clock. Bend your right knee, so it is above your ankle. This protects your knee. Inhale your arms to Warrior 2 by extending your right arm forward and left arm back to shoulder height. Your gaze can be over the middle finger of your right hand. If this creates tension in your neck, slightly rotate it to the left until your neck feels open and free.

Take a few deep, calm breaths, mentally affirming **"I am grounded and connected to the earth"**. Feel that you are supported by the earth.

Change sides and enjoy this pose on this side.

Benefits:

- Strengthens the legs, ankles, hips, while also stretching the groin, chest, and shoulders
- It can help improve concentration, determination, and focus.
- Improves balance and reduces falls.
- Reduces low back pain.
- Increases leg strength and endurance.
- Reduces stress and anxiety.

Chair option: Sit on a chair with the chair back on your right side. Your right knee is directly underneath your hip.

Keep your right hip on the chair and slide your left foot back. Slightly bring your left hip forward and right hip back. Inhale, as you raise your right arm forward and left arm back, and take a few deep, slow breaths here. If you feel stable, pressing the toes and ball of your back foot into the earth, you could raise both arms, and take a few deep, slow breaths here.

Mentally affirm **"I am grounded and connected to the earth"**.

Change sides and enjoy this pose on this side.

Mudra: **Life force** (Prana) **Mudra**

Place the tips of your thumb, ring and little fingers together with each hand. Extend your index and middle fingers out straight, touching. Rest your hands on your legs. Mentally affirm **"I am grounded and connected to the earth"**.

Pranayama:

Cross legged, place your hands on shoulders, inhale through nose, arms up, knees towards each other, exhale through mouth, hands to shoulders, knees wide.

Repeat 16 times. Now relax your arms, and return to your regular breath.

Notice how grounded and connected to the earth you feel.

2nd chakra: Svadhisthana (Sacral)

Element: **Water** **Chant:** **Vam**

Affirmation: **"I express my creativity freely."**

Asana: **Wide legged forward bend** (Prasarita Padottanasana)

From standing, step your feet wide apart with your feet as parallel as comfortable. Place your hands on your hips. Inhale and lengthen your spine, exhale, as you draw the belly in towards the spine and slowly fold forward from the hips half of the way, keeping your spine long. It is ok to round your back now, to place your hands on the earth underneath your shoulders. Make sure your legs are engaged and head and neck are relaxed.

Take a few deep, peaceful breaths, mentally affirming **"I express my creativity freely"**, whichever affirmation feels most beneficial for you at this time. Enjoy a calm mind that will flow through changes gracefully. Place your hands on your hips. Engage your belly, and inhale up with a straight spine. Step your feet together.

Benefits:

- Stretches the hamstrings, inner thighs, and groins, improving flexibility in the lower body.
- Relieves tension in the lower back and spine by elongating the muscles and promoting relaxation.
- Stimulates the abdominal organs, aiding digestion and promoting detoxification.
- Calms the mind, reduces stress, encourages introspection and mindfulness.
- Strengthens the quadriceps and calves.
- Improves posture and alignment by lengthening the spine and opening the chest and shoulders.

- Promotes a sense of grounding and stability by connecting the body with the earth.
- Can help alleviate menstrual discomfort and symptoms of menopause.
- Enhances circulation throughout the body, promoting overall cardiovascular health.

Asana: **Revolved Triangle** (Parivrtta Trikonasana)

From standing, step your left foot back, Place your left hand on the outside of your right foot (or on a block or thick book or leg). On the inhalation, engage your belly to protect your lower back, spiral to the right, and raise your right arm up. Look up if this is expansive for your neck. If this creates tension in your neck, look down.

Enjoy a few deep, slow breaths, mentally affirming **"I express my creativity freely"**. Exhale your right arm down. Engage your belly and slowly come up with a flat spine. Step your left foot forward to meet the right.

Change sides, and enjoy this pose on this side.

Benefits:

- Opens up the chest, shoulders, hamstrings, and hips, enhancing flexibility in these areas.
- Engages and strengthens the legs, core muscles, and spine, promoting stability and balance.
- Stimulates the abdominal organs, aiding in digestion and promoting detoxification.
- Provides a deep twist to the spine, helping to increase mobility and relieve tension in the back and to wring out toxins from the organs and tissues, supporting overall detoxification.
- Enhances Focus and Concentration.
- Promotes the release of stagnant energy in the body, revitalizing and invigorating the yogi.
- Balances Nervous System, inducing a sense of calm and relaxation.

- Improves Posture, encourages proper spinal alignment and posture, reducing the risk of back pain and injury.
- Cultivates mindfulness and self-awareness

Asana: **Downward facing dog** (Adho Mukha Svanasana)

On hands and knees your hands are directly under your shoulders, knees are under your hips. On the exhalation extend your legs and lift your knees. Your palms are pressing into the earth, middle fingers facing forward. Your hips are high, and your neck is relaxed.

Take several deep, slow breaths, mentally affirming **"I express my creativity freely"**.

Return to your hands and knees.

Benefits:

- Improves hamstring flexibility.
- Reduces lower back pain as well as frequency and intensity of migraines.
- Improves respiratory function.
- Improves bone density and can reduce pain and stiffness in individuals with knee osteoarthritis
- Improves grip strength and reduced pain intensity in individuals with carpal tunnel syndrome.

Mudra: **Shakti Mudra**

Benefits:

- **Calms the mind** and soothes the nervous system.
- Improves **sleep patterns** and helps with insomnia.
- Enhances **inner strength** and stability.
- Boosts **internal energy** and improves overall health.
- Specifically targets the **pelvic region**, reducing tension and discomfort.
- Aids in healing weaknesses within the body.

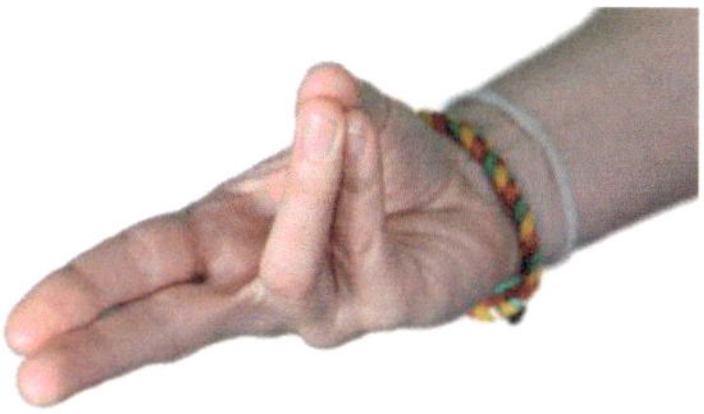

With your palms in front of your chest, press your pinky and ring fingertips together. Fold your thumbs into your palms, inside of your index and middle finger. You can then press the knuckles of these two fingers together or keep them separate.

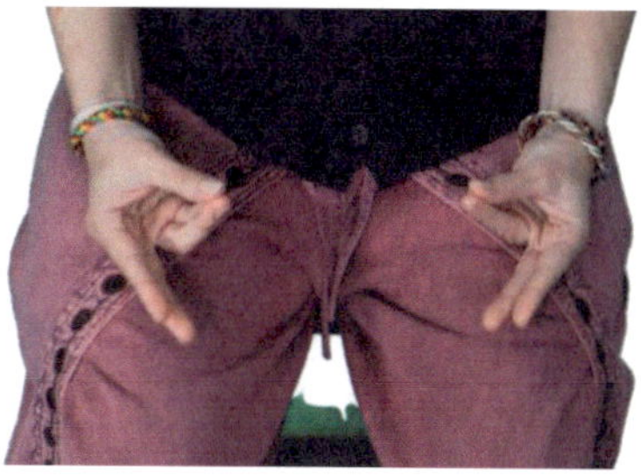

Optional step: Lower the hands to just below the navel.

Mentally affirm **"I express my creativity freely"**.

Pranayama: **Victorious Breath** (Ujjayi) (no image necessary)

Inhale and exhale through the nose with a slightly restricted throat, creating a soft ocean-like sound.

Notice how free you feel to express your creativity.

3rd chakra: Manipura (Solar Plexus)

Element: **Fire**

Chant: **Ram**

Affirmation: **"I digest (life) with ease and grace."**

Asana: **Boat** (Navasana)

Sit with your knees bent and your feet flat on the earth. Lean back, tuck your tailbone, and lift your legs, bent or straight. It is easier to have the legs bent. Extend your arms forward.

Take a few deep, slow breaths, mentally affirming **"I digest (life) with ease and grace"**.

Feel that you are cultivating empowerment. Lower your feet to the earth and sit up straight.

Benefits:

- Engages and strengthens the abdominal muscles and legs.
- Improves Balance and stability.
- Stretches the hip flexors, aiding in relieving tightness in this area.
- Promotes a strong and healthy spine by encouraging proper alignment and posture.
- Activates the digestive system, massaging the organs and improving digestion.
- Enhances focus and concentration, fostering mental clarity and presence.
- Increases confidence as yogis challenge themselves to hold the pose and extend their capabilities.
- Boosts energy levels and invigorates the body, making it a great pose for waking up and starting the day.

Asana: **Wind removing pose** (Pavanamuktasana)

Lying on your back, draw both knees in towards your chest. Clasp your hands a couple of inches below your right knee. Straighten your left leg onto the earth. With every exhalation draw your right knee in towards your right shoulder, avoiding the ribcage. This activates the ascending colon.

Take at least 10 deep, slow breaths, mentally affirming **"I digest life with ease and grace"**. Relax your right leg, straighten it onto the earth.

Change sides, drawing the left knee into the left shoulder activates the descending colon.

After at least ten slow breaths, focusing on your affirmation, release your leg.

Draw both knees in towards your chest. Hug your knees and hold onto the opposite elbow or hand. With every exhalation, lengthen your spine, keep it extended and draw the knees in towards your chest.

Take at least ten slow breaths, focusing on your affirmation. Relax your arms and legs, extend both legs on the earth.

Feel fresh, healing energy flow through your digestive system.

Benefits:

- Compresses the abdomen, stimulating digestion, promoting the elimination of waste and toxins, and relieving gas and bloating.
- Stretches the hip flexor muscles, reducing tightness in the hips.
- Provides a gentle stretch to the lower back muscles, relieving tension and discomfort.
- Increases flexibility in the hip joints and lower spine, enhancing overall range of motion.
- Promotes relaxation and stress relief.

Asana: **Bow** (Dhanurasana)

Lying on your belly with your legs hip distance apart, exhale while bending your knees. Lift your upper body up off the earth. Reach your right hand back and hold onto the outside of your right ankle. Reach your left hand back and hold onto the outside of your left ankle. You can just reach your arms back if it is challenging to touch your ankles. Gently lift your thighs away from the earth.

Take five deep, slow breaths, mentally affirming **"I digest life with ease and grace"**.

Let go of your ankles. **Exhale, as you slowly roll onto your belly.**

Benefits:

- Stretches the front of the body, including the abdomen, chest, and thighs.
- Strengthens the back muscles, including the erector spinae and rhomboids.
- Improves flexibility and mobility in the spine.
- Stimulates the digestive organs, aiding digestion and elimination.
- Opens the shoulders, releases tension and stress in the back and shoulders and improves posture.
- Enhances lung capacity and respiratory function.
- Promotes balance and coordination.
- Energizes the body and increases vitality.

Mudra: **Matangi Mudra**

Interlace all fingers of both hands, extend your middle fingers up to touch, and hold at the solar plexus, two inches above your navel. Mentally affirm **"I digest life with ease and grace"**.

Feel free to hold this mudra as you practice the following pranayama.

Pranayama: **Breath of Fire, also called Skull Shining Breath** (Kapalbhati) (no image necessary)

Breathe in through the nose, exhale sharply through the nose while drawing the belly in towards the spine, repeat 16 times or more.

If you get dizzy, return to regular breath. Start with fewer repetitions and build up over time.

Trust that, as you move forward in life, you will digest your experiences with ease and grace.

4th chakra: Anahata (Heart)

Element: Air

Chant: Yam

Affirmation: **"I am love."**

Asana: **High lunge** (Utthita Ashwa Sanchalanasana)

From hands and knees, step your right foot forward between your hands. Your knee is directly above your ankle. Tuck the back toes under and straighten your left leg. You could keep your back knee on the earth for more stability. Engage your belly and inhale your torso and arms up.

Lengthen and take a few deep, slow breaths here, mentally affirming **"I am love"**.

You could exhale your arms into cactus by bending them 90 degrees at the elbows to open your heart.

Inhale your arms up, exhale your arms into cactus. You could bend your back knee with each exhalation and straighten with the inhalation for a more dynamic flow. Feel it out for your own body.

Exhale your hands to either side of your front foot, return to hands and knees.

Change sides and enjoy this pose on this side.

Benefits:

- Opens and stretches the hip flexors, including the psoas and iliopsoas muscles.
- Builds strength in the quadriceps, hamstrings, and calf muscles.

- Enhances balance and stability, especially when engaging the core muscles.
- Expands the chest and stretches the shoulders, relieving tension and promoting better posture.
- Increases flexibility in the hips, thighs, and groin area.
- Provides a gentle cardiovascular workout, increasing circulation and boosting energy levels.
- Requires concentration and mindfulness to maintain balance and alignment, improving mental focus.
- Relieves tension in the lower back and improves overall spinal mobility.

Asana: **Cobra** (Bhujangasana)

Lying on your belly, place your hands on the earth, close to your chest, with elbows close to your body. Inhale, pressing into your palms, keeping your elbows bent, and lift your upper body. You can use your back muscles to lift higher.

Breathe with love in this beautiful heart opener, mentally affirming **"I am love"**..

After a few mindful breaths, slowly exhale down.

Benefits:

- Strengthens the back, shoulders, and arms while also stretching the chest and lungs.
- It can also help improve posture.
- Reduces low back pain.
- Increases spinal mobility.
- Reduces stress and anxiety.
- Improves lung function.

Asana: **Upward facing dog** (Urdhva Mukha Svanasana)

From Cobra, extend your arms and roll your shoulders back into a deeper heart opener. Leading from the heart, breathe with love, mentally affirming **"I am love"**.

After several slow breaths, slowly exhale down onto your belly.

Benefits:

- Stretches the chest, shoulders, and abdomen.
- Strengthens the arms, wrists, and spine.
- Improves posture and spinal alignment.
- Stimulates abdominal organs and improves digestion.
- Opens the heart center, promoting emotional well-being.
- Increases energy and vitality.
- Improves respiratory function by expanding the chest and lungs.
- Enhances flexibility in the spine and back muscles.

Mudra: **Lotus Mudra**

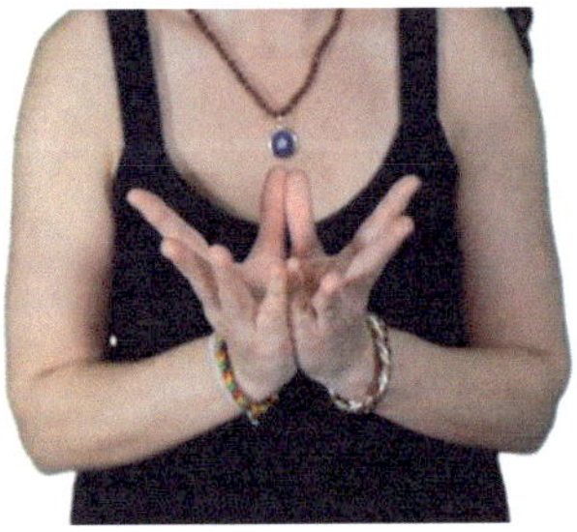

With your palms at your heart, touch the outer edges of both pinky fingers and thumbs together. Keep the heels of the palms pressed together as you blossom open through your hands.

Extend through the tips of all 10 fingers.

Mentally affirm **"I am love"**.

Feel free to hold this mudra as you practice the following pranayama.

Pranayama: **Anahata Pranayama** (no image necessary)

Sit comfortably in a cross-legged position or on a chair with your spine straight and shoulders relaxed. Close your eyes and take a few deep breaths to center yourself.

Place your hands on your heart center (the center of your chest).

Inhale deeply into your heart chakra through the nose slowly, mentally affirming **"I am love"**. Feel love in your heart.

Exhale slowly and completely through your nose, feeling the release of any tension or negativity from your heart.

Continue this rhythmic breathing, focusing on the rise and fall of your chest and the sensation of energy flowing to your heart center.

As you breathe, visualize a soft green light surrounding your heart, symbolizing love, compassion, and healing energy.

Stay in this practice for several minutes, allowing yourself to connect with the energy of your heart center and cultivate feelings of love and compassion towards yourself and others.

Regular practice of Anahata Pranayama can help open and balance the heart chakra, promoting emotional well-being, compassion, and harmonious relationships.

5th chakra: Vissudha (Throat)

Element: Ether **Chant: Ham**

Affirmation: "I express truth with clarity."

Asana: Pyramid (Parsvottanasana)

From standing, step your left foot slightly back, both legs straight. Place your hands at your hips, hinge forward half way with a flat back, then round in. Place your finger tips or hands on either side of your front foot. You can use blocks or thick books. Bring your throat to your chest to feel a sense of compression in the throat. This is a wonderful pose to balance your thyroid.

Take a few deep, slow breaths, affirming mentally **"I express truth with clarity"**.

Inhale your hands to your hips, engage our belly, and lift your torso. Step your left foot forward to meet the right. Relax your arms.

Change sides, and enjoy this pose on this side.

Benefits:

- Lengthens and stretches the muscles at the back of the thighs, improving flexibility and range of motion.
- Provides a gentle stretch to the hip flexors and groin muscles, promoting hip flexibility.
- Engages the quadriceps and calf muscles, building strength and stability in the legs.
- Helps correct alignment issues by elongating the spine and encouraging proper posture.

- Activates the abdominal organs, including the liver and kidneys, supporting digestion and detoxification.
- Challenges balance and concentration, improving mental focus and presence.
- Alleviates tension in the lower back by elongating the spine and releasing tightness in the muscles.
- Promotes a sense of calm and relaxation by focusing on breath awareness and mindful movement.

Asana: **Camel** (Ustrasana)

Only practice Camel after you have warmed up your spine with some gentle forward and back bends, such as Pyramid or Cat-Cow.

From hands and knees, lift your upper body on the inhalation. Place your hands on your lower back, fingers facing down. Inhale and lengthen your spine, exhale, slowly bend back. Breathe slowly and deeply affirming mentally **"I express truth with clarity"**.

If you like a deeper expression, your right hand could reach back and hold onto your right ankle. Your left hand could reach back and hold onto your left ankle. Keep your head in alignment with your neck and spine.

Take a few deep breaths, affirming mentally **"I express truth with clarity"**. Inhale, tucking your chin towards the chest, lift your right hand to your lower back, your left hand to your lower back. Supporting your back, slowly inhale your torso up. Exhale to your hands and knees.

Benefits:

- Opens and stretches the chest, shoulders, and front of the body.
- Improves posture and helps counteract the effects of prolonged sitting.
- Strengthens the back muscles and improves spinal flexibility.
- Enhances lung capacity and deep breathing.
- May relieve mild backaches and reduce tension in the neck and shoulders.

Asana: **Lion** (Simhasana)

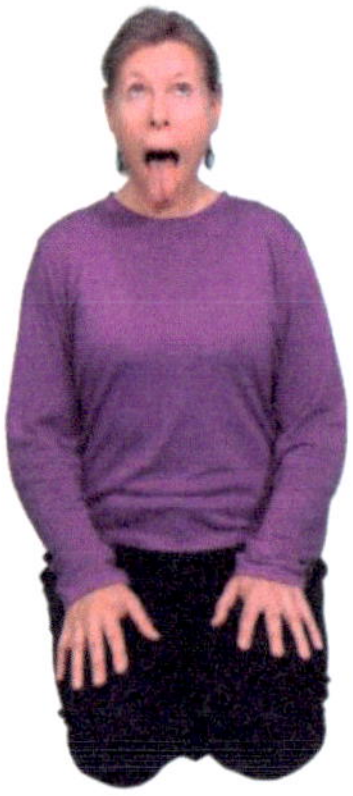

Sit with your hips on your heels and palms resting on your knees or legs or sit on a chair. Inhale and reach the top of your head up to lengthen your spine. Arch your spine, look up at your third eye, your intuitive center between your eyebrows, stretch your tongue out and down and exhale through the mouth, roaring like a lion with a "haaa" sound. Inhale to starting position and repeat three-five timcs, mentally affirming **"I express truth with clarity"**. Feel how open and clear your throat chakra is.

Benefits:

- Relieves tension in the face, throat, and neck.
- Releases stress and promotes relaxation.
- Stimulates facial muscles and improves facial expression.
- Helps reduce anxiety and improves mood.
- May relieve symptoms of mild throat and voice-related disorders.

Mudra: **Granthita (Knot) Mudra**

Interlace your last three fingers (middle, ring, and pinky) together. Interlock the index fingertips and thumbs to form two rings, and hold this mudra in front of the base of your throat. Mentally affirm **"I express truth with clarity"**. Feel free to hold this mudra as you practice the following pranayama.

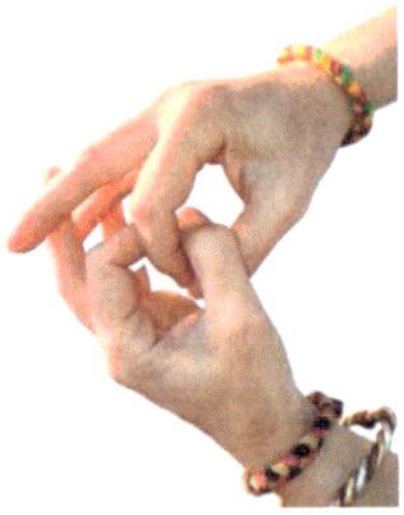

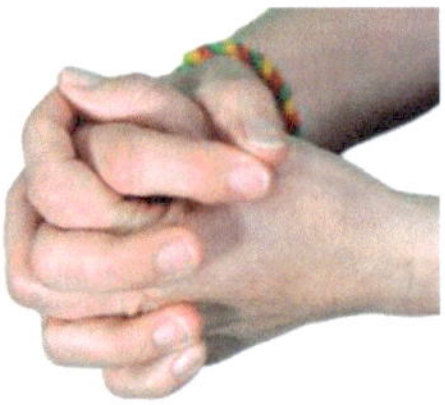

Pranayama: **Ujjayi (Victorious) Breath:** (no image necessary)

Inhale and exhale through the nose with a slightly restricted throat, creating a soft ocean-like sound. Repeat at least 10 times. **Notice how clear your throat feels and how safe and empowered you feel to express truth.**

6th chakra: Ajna (Third Eye)

Element: **Light** **Chant:** **Aum**

Affirmation: **"I am divinely guided."**

Asana: **Gate** (Parighasana)

From kneeling. stretch your left leg out to the side. Your heel touches the earth and toes point up. Inhale your right arm up above your head and exhale it towards the left, opening the gate from the material to the spiritual world. Allow your left hand to slide down along your left leg. Make sure you lean to the left, not forward. It can be a subtle movement. Take a few deep, slow breaths, mentally affirming **"I am divinely guided"**. Create some space on the inhalation; allow the exhalation to gently deepen the pose. Inhale your arms up, exhale down alongside your body as you come to the starting position.

Change sides, and enjoy this pose on this side.

Benefits:

- Stretches and strengthens the side body, hips, and hamstrings.
- Improves flexibility and range of motion in the torso.
- Relieves tension and tightness in the back and hips.
- Enhances digestion and stimulates abdominal organs.

Chair option: Sit on a chair, and enjoy the same asana as described above on both sides.

Asana: **Dolphin** (Ardha Pincha Mayurasana)

Start in downward facing dog. Now rest the elbows, forearms and palms down on the floor. The elbows are in line with the shoulders and feet are about hip width apart. Firm your shoulder blades towards each other and exhale your shoulders away from the ears to free your neck.

Press the hips up into the sky and move your heels towards the earth. They do not need to touch the earth. Keep your gaze gently lifted to your third eye. Your neck is relaxed.

Enjoy a few deep, slow breaths here, mentally affirming **"I am divinely guided"**.

Bring all of your attention to the third eye.

Benefits:

- Strengthens the shoulders, arms, and upper back muscles, including the deltoids, triceps, and rhomboids.
- Stretches and lengthens the shoulder muscles and chest, enhancing flexibility and mobility in the shoulder joints.
- Creates traction along the spine, decompressing the vertebrae and lengthening the entire length of the spine.
- Alleviates mild back pain and discomfort by gently stretching and releasing tension in the back muscles.
- Expands the chest and rib cage, improving respiratory function and promoting deeper breathing.
- Promotes relaxation and reduces stress and anxiety by calming the nervous system and focusing the mind.
- Builds strength and stability in the shoulders and core, preparing the body for more advanced inversions like headstand and forearm stand.

Asana: **Eagle** (Garudasana)

From Mountain Pose, standing with both feet hip distance apart, arms alongside your body, inhale your arms up above your head. Exhale your right elbow under your left. Your palms may touch or move towards each other. Maintaining this pose, inhale your arms up to feel a stretch in your shoulders.

Take a few breaths. mentally affirming **"I am divinely guided"**.

Exhale your elbows down. Bend your knees, wrap your right knee over the left knee. Your toes can touch the ground on the outside of your left foot, or you can wrap your right foot around your left ankle. Squeeze under your ankles, ground, armpits, elbow and wrists to activate the lymphatic system.

Take a few breaths, silently repeating with your affirmation.

Relax your arms and legs and return to Mountain Pose. Enjoy a few breaths here.

Change sides, and enjoy this pose on this side.

Benefits:

- Improves balance and stability by strengthening your legs, ankles, and feet.
- Reduces stress and anxiety, the pose can help to calm the mind.
- Enhances concentration requiring you to pay close attention to your body and breath.
- Stretches and tones muscles helping to stretch and tone the muscles in your legs, hips, and shoulders.
- Boosts energy and reduces fatigue.
- Improves digestion by stimulating the digestive system.
- Relieves tension in the neck.

Chair and floor option: Perform the pose as described above seated on a chair or lying on your back.

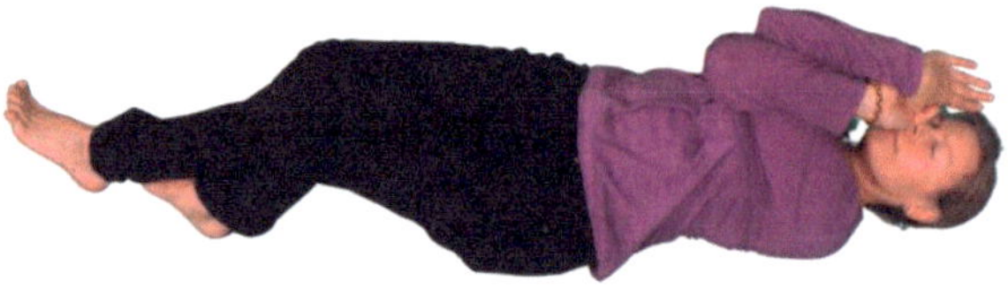

Asana: **Child's Pose** (Balasana)

Kneel and sit on your heels. Lean forward, keeping your buttocks on your heels, and rest your forehead on the earth. Bring your arms alongside your body with palms facing up to receive.

Take a few deep, slow breaths, mentally affirming **"I am divinely guided"**.

Gently move your head from side to side, massaging and activating your third eye.

Benefits:

- A relaxing pose that can help reduce stress and tension in the body.
- It stretches the hips, thighs, and ankles.
- Reduces stress and anxiety
- Reduces low back pain
- Increases spinal flexibility
- Improves sleep quality

Mudra: **3rd Eye Chakra Mudra** (Mudra of the Great Head)

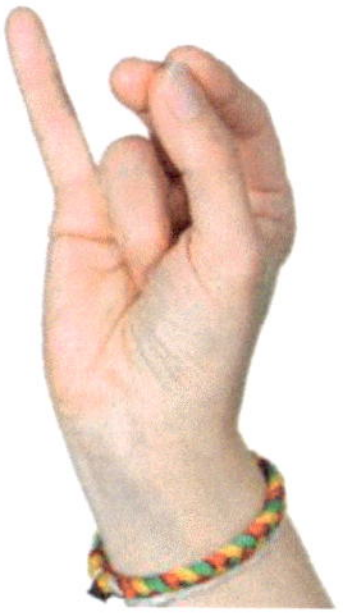

Take your right hand just in front of the space between your eyebrows and curl the ring finger into your palm. Bring the tips of the thumb, middle finger, and index finger to touch, and keep the pinky finger extended long. Place the tips of the three fingers that are touching to your third-eye focal point. The left hand can remain on top of the left thigh, palm face-up.

Mentally affirm **"I am divinely guided"**.

Pranayama: **Alternate nostril breathing** (Nadi Shodhana)

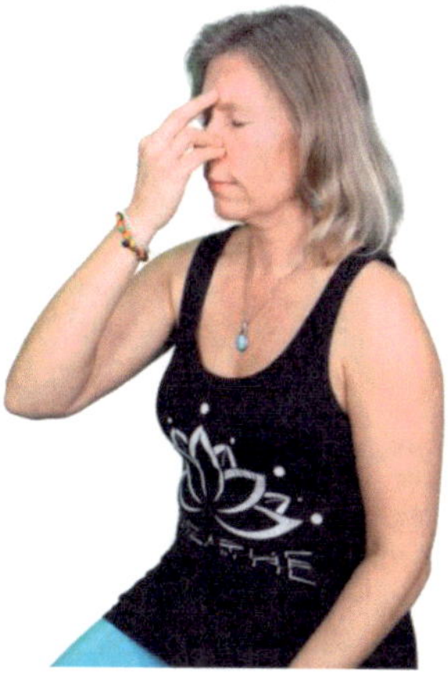

This powerful breathing technique brings balance to the right and left hemispheres of your brain.

Raise your right hand and rest your index finger and middle finger on your forehead at your Third Eye Chakra. Let your thumb rest on your right nostril. Rest your ring finger and little finger on your left nostril.

Block your right nostril with your thumb and inhale through your left nostril.

Next, block your left nostril and release your thumb to exhale through your right nostril. Keep the breath out for a few seconds.

Alternate this pattern of breathing from left to right and then right to left 10 to 15 times.

You are now clear to receive divine guidance.

7th chakra: Sahasrara (Crown)

Element: **Thought** **Chant:** **AUM**

Affirmation: **"I am divine"**

Asana: **Shoulder stand** (Salamba Sarvangasana)

If you have neck imbalances, please avoid shoulder stand. Lift your legs up against a wall instead. You will receive the same benefits.

For shoulder stand lie on your back with a folded blanket or towel under your upper back and shoulders. Your head and neck are off the blanket or towel. Place your feet on the earth, Your arms are by your side, palms facing down. Inhale while lifting up your legs. Press into your forearms to lift your hips and lower back.

Place your hands on your lower back and extend one leg up, then the other. Avoid moving your head to the sides.

Keep your gaze upward and your neck straight. Lift up through the balls of your feet, walking your hands up along your back. Enjoy a few deep, slow breaths, mentally affirming **"I am divine"**.

From here move into Plough pose, as described below. Avoid Plough if you experience pain in the neck.

Benefits:

- Strengthens the core, shoulders, and neck muscles.
- Improves posture and body alignment.
- Increases blood flow to the brain, enhancing mental clarity.
- Promotes thyroid health and stimulates the endocrine system.
- Calms the nervous system and helps relieve stress

Asana: **Plough** (Halasana)

If shoulder stand does not feel right to your body at this time, please avoid Plough. Bring your legs up the wall instead.

To practice Plough: From shoulder stand, bring one leg behind your head while supporting your back with your hands, then the other leg. Ideally your legs are straight. If your toes touch the earth, you can clasp your hands behind your back, straighten your arms and lower the knuckles to the earth towards the front of your mat.

Your throat will feel slightly restricted, which is beneficial for the thyroid. Take a few deep, slow breaths. mentally affirming **"I am divine"**.

Place your arms onto the earth alongside your body, palms facing down. Inhale one leg up, then the other. Slowly roll your spine down on the exhalation, one vertebra at a time. Slowly lower your legs down, keeping them straight. If you feel pain in your lower back, bend your knees as you lower your legs.

Benefits:

- Increases flexibility and mobility in the entire length of the spine, particularly the cervical (neck) and thoracic (upper back) regions.
- Stretches and lengthens the muscles along the back of the body, including the erector spinae and trapezius muscles.
- Provides gentle compression to the throat area, stimulating the thyroid gland and regulating its function.
- Promotes relaxation and reduces stress and anxiety by calming the nervous system.
- Stimulates the abdominal organs, including the liver and pancreas, aiding in digestion and promoting detoxification.
- Alleviates mild back pain and discomfort by decompressing the spinal vertebrae and releasing tension in the back muscles.
- Increases blood circulation to the brain and neck region, nourishing the nerves and enhancing mental clarity.
- Relieves insomnia and promotes restful sleep by calming the mind and reducing tension in the body.

Asana: **Legs up the wall option**

Lie on your back facing a wall with knees bent. Your buttocks are close to the wall. Extend your legs up against the wall, and enjoy a few deep, slow breaths in this inversion. mentally affirming **“I am divine”**.

Blood and oxygen are flowing to your heart and crown, activating your crown chakra.

Can be practiced as a restorative pose to rejuvenate the body and mind after a long day, or following intense physical activity, and to help alleviate insomnia.

Benefits:

- Promotes relaxation and relieves stress, promoting mental clarity and emotional balance.
- Improves circulation by allowing blood to flow more easily from the feet and legs back to the heart.
- Reduces swelling in the lower extremities by facilitating lymphatic drainage.
- Alleviates tension in the legs, lower back, and hips, and increases flexibility and mobility.
- Helps to relieve mild back pain and discomfort.
- May help to alleviate symptoms of mild anxiety and depression.

Asana: **Supine twist** (Supta Matsyendrasana)

Lying on your back, bend your knees, and place your feet on the earth. Press into your feet, lift your hips and rest them on the earth about one inch to the right. With the exhalation draw your right knee in towards your chest while extending your left leg out in front of you on the earth. with your left foot flexed.

Inhale, and with the next exhalation place your left hand on your right knee, and exhale the knee towards the earth on the left side of your body. Open your right arm to the right. Turn your head to the right.

IF this creates tension in your neck, bring your head to the center. Enjoy a few deep, slow breaths. mentally affirming **"I am divine"**. Inhale your knee and arm to center, exhale while extending your leg on the earth. Rest for a few breaths.

Change sides, and enjoy this pose on this side.

Benefits:

- Increases flexibility and mobility in the spine, particularly the thoracic and lumbar regions.
- Helps release tension and stiffness in the back muscles, promoting relaxation and comfort.
- Stimulates the digestive organs, including the stomach and intestines, aiding in digestion and relieving bloating.
- Eases lower back pain by gently stretching and elongating the muscles surrounding the lumbar spine.
- Facilitates the elimination of toxins and waste products from the body by stimulating lymphatic drainage.
- Promotes relaxation and reduces stress, anxiety, and fatigue by calming the nervous system.
- Enhances blood circulation to the spine and surrounding muscles, supporting their health and function.
- Encourages deep breathing and diaphragmatic movement, enhancing oxygenation and promoting a sense of well-being.

Asana: **Corpse Pose** (Shavasana)

This pose may seem "uneventful", yet it is often considered the most important pose of all. This is your opportunity to integrate all benefits of yoga into your whole being.

Lying on your back, separate your legs slightly. You may choose to widen your legs as much as feels comfortable. Allow your toes to relax out to the sides. Relax your arms, palms facing up, by your sides, slightly away from your torso. Tuck your shoulder blades in towards each other to open your heart and shoulders. Completely relax and let go.

Just breathe calmly with **"I am divine"** and allow yourself to "melt" into the earth. You may let go of the affirmation when your mind is calm. **Just be!**

Enjoy this pose for ten minutes. Deep healing often occurs in stillness. **Allow it!**

Benefits:

- Helps reduce stress and tension in the body.
- Can improve focus and concentration.
- Can reduce fatigue and anxiety.
- Reduces anxiety and depression.
- Improves sleep quality.
- Reduces blood pressure.

Mudra: **Mudra of a Thousand Petals**

Place the tips of both index fingers and tips of both thumbs together to touch, forming a pyramid shape. Allow the remaining fingers to extend upward, keeping them straight.

Raise this mudra to about six to seven inches above the crown of your head. Mentally affirm **"I am divine"**.

Pranayama: Double Breathing (with tension)

Enjoy a double breath in through the nose.

Hold the breath while making fists with your hands and tensing all the muscles of your whole body.

Double breath out through the mouth, as you relax completely.

Repeat five times or as many times as you need to feel completely relaxed.

Feel your divine nature.

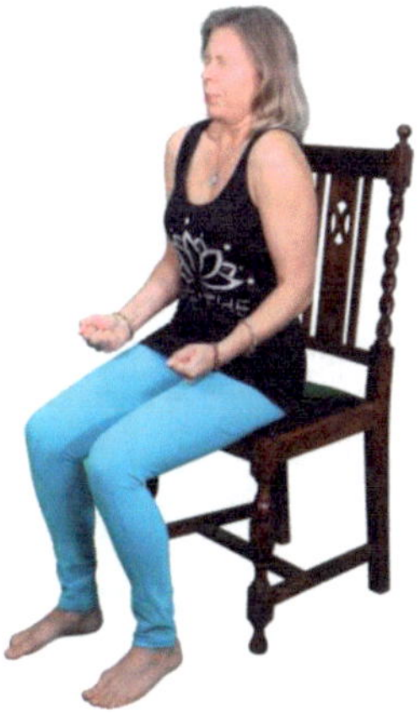

My Personal Morning Flow

I am guided to share with you my morning flow that I have been practicing, almost automatically, every day for many years. I am sharing it as an example for what you can enjoy for yourself.

No matter how busy I may be, this is what I do no matter what. It offers amazing benefits to my whole being. It opens and balances my body, mind, spirit and soul, and creates a wonderful empowering, peaceful foundation for the day.

- Yogananda's Energization Exercises (you can learn about them if you sign up for lessons on www.yogananda.org or www.ananda.org)
- Wind removing pose
- Prone figure four
- Sit-ups
- Prone airplane
- On belly, lifting and extending one arm forward and opposite leg back
- Cat-cow, then with arm and leg extended on inhalation, rounding in with breath of fire on exhalation
- Sun salutation
- High lunge with twist
- Tree and/or dancer
- Boat
- Bow
- Shoulder stand
- Plough
- Rabbit
- Supine twist
- Rock pose (sitting on heels) for alternate nostril breathing with Gyan mudra (thumbs and index fingers touching)
- Meditation

Throughout the day I practice additional asanas that I am guided to. On most days I enjoy a bike ride, beach walk, swim or run, and a few times per week I lift light weights.

Build *YOUR* Personal Morning Flow

After experiencing all the tools in this book, **what morning flow are you committing to for yourself?**

What feels opening, nourishing, strengthening and balancing to you? In yoga, ideally we move the spine in all the different directions, forward, back, sides and twists.

What mudras and pranayama's will you include?

Create YOUR morning flow here:

Just do it - regularly!

It will enhance your well-being and focus and inspire people around you.

To an End of a Life in Pain

Life is simple, only our mind tries to make it complicated. All we have is this present moment. The past is over, the future is unknown, the Now is the only reality. Focus on this moment. Enjoy the simple pleasures of life and don't get caught up in the material world, pain, and struggle.

Watch a sunrise or sunset, enjoy the beauty and perfection of one single flower, gaze into the sky and observe the clouds, hear the sound of leaves in the breeze, listen to the soothing sound of a river or the ocean, indulge in your favorite healthy meal and truly savor it, lay on your sofa and be thankful for your safe home, for everything and everyone you have in your life at this time. Be grateful for all of your experiences, as they have brought you to where you are today. Feel joy, be happy, bathe in gratitude, be in awe of the power of the universe and the fact that you are part of it and indulge in deep inner peace. Love yourself with your imperfections.

I am honored to be part of your journey into happiness and peace. May you be blessed and have the courage, trust and faith to listen to your heart, follow your heart's guidance, and commit to live your purpose passionately, to feel good, be happy, and at peace.

I trust that our paths will cross again, possibly when you are ready to take your commitment to the next level and are looking for support which you may find in my meditation and yoga CD's, Yoga and ThetaHealing® sessions and workshops in person and online, or future books. Let's stay in touch.

From the light in my heart to the light in your heart, I bow to you. Namaste.

In Divine Friendship,

Anke

In Gratitude

I honor and am grateful for all the beings - people, animals and spirits - that have helped me to become who I am today and to inspire me to give birth to this book.

My parents Werner and Gisela Banderski hold a very special place in my life and heart for the stable foundation they provide me throughout this life.

My Supreme Guru, Paramhansa Yogananda, whose Divine Love, wisdom, and deep guidance at all times has afforded me the Grace to always seek God in all things, large and small. In His words "The time to know God is NOW!"

And to my life-partner Casey Hughes, for co-creating our beautiful, sacred life together, bringing his boundless creativity, vision, and editing skills to this book.

My Spiritual Family throughout the world, you have inspired me, loved me, shown me, through your own lives, how to deepen my attunement to God and Guru. And I remain forever grateful for the lessons from my Guru, engaged through his organization the Self Realization Fellowship, integrated with the teaching and kriya practice brought through Gurudev's direct disciple Swami Kriyananda and my Gurubais living among the many global Spiritual Communities of Ananda. All have shaped my life, and accelerated the ever expanding consciousness which I strive for.

In my own life journey towards "No Pain, All Gain", I was fortunate to encounter Vianna Stibal, whose creative force manifested the ThetaHealing practice which has opened countless doors for me, personally and professionally (www.ThetaHealing.com).

And the guy on the street in New York who suggested yoga to me in the first place, I bow in humble gratitude.

To those now reading this expression of sincere gratitude, I say "thank you" for even considering experiencing and perhaps internalizing the essence of this book. May it bring you "No Pain, All Gain"!

And to all my clients for inspiring and informing the creation of this book and the refinement of my personal and professional healing practices..

Thank you one and all for being open, ready, willing, and committed to enhance the world through your own personal transformation.

Research & References

Research and reference citations are simply too numerous and extensive to be included effectively within ***"No Pain All Gain"***.

For those interested, we have compiled an extensive Bibliography available freely from our website.

All practices included in *"No Pain All Gain"* , and their relative studies supporting their efficacy referenced within this book have been peer-reviewed and published in reputable scientific journals.

While these studies provide increasing support for the use of yoga practices (esp. affirmations, asanas, pranayama, and mudras) as complementary therapies for wellness and pain management, more research is needed to fully understand their effects and how they might be best incorporated into a comprehensive wellness and pain management plan. It's important to note that yoga practices (affirmations, asanas, pranayama, and mudras) should not be used as a substitute for medical treatment, but rather as a supplement to other pain management strategies recommended by a healthcare professional.

These studies and their related citations are all listed at **www.ReleaseIntoBliss.com/BookResearch** and comprise a detailed Bibliography for "No Pain, All Gain" with each citation listed in APA style.

The type of yoga used in the studies cited within "No Pain All Gain" and its Bibliography vary. Most of the studies used Hatha yoga or a modified version of Hatha yoga, which is a gentle form of yoga that focuses on breathing, relaxation, and holding physical postures. Some studies also used Iyengar yoga, which is a form of Hatha yoga that emphasizes alignment and uses props to support the body in the postures. Other types of yoga used in some studies included Viniyoga, Restorative yoga, and Kundalini yoga.

The yogic practices, and the entirety of discourses offered the reader within "No Pain, All Gain", represent the broadest, most comprehensive system of yoga, referred to as Raja Yoga. Built upon the platform of Ashtanga, the 8-fold path originally formulated by the great Indian Sage Patanjali, who documented the modern system of yoga in the Yoga Sutras. The term "ashtanga" is derived from Sanskrit, where "ashta" means "eight," and "anga" means "limbs" or "steps." These eight limbs serve as a comprehensive guide for ethical and spiritual living, leading to self-realization and liberation.

Glossary

5-Pointed Star pose (Utthita Tadasana): A standing yoga posture where the practitioner stands with their feet wide apart and arms extended out to the sides, creating a five-pointed star shape. It stretches the body and promotes balance.

Abraham (Estimated 2000 BCE): A central figure in Judaism, Christianity, and Islam, known for his covenant with God and considered the patriarch of these religions.

Ahura Mazda (Approximately 6th century BCE): The highest deity in Zoroastrianism, symbolizing truth, order, and goodness, and is often depicted as a wise figure.

Amma: A term for a mother figure, also associated with Mata Amritanandamayi, a spiritual leader known as the "Hugging Saint" for her practice of embracing people to convey love and compassion.

Anjali: A Sanskrit term for the gesture of bringing palms together at the heart center, often accompanied by a slight bow, symbolizing respect, gratitude, and unity.

APA Citation Style: A format for citing sources in academic writing according to the guidelines set by the American Psychological Association (APA), commonly used in social sciences and other fields.

Applied Kinesiology: A diagnostic technique combining principles from chiropractic and muscle testing to assess health by evaluating muscle strength and function.

Asanas: Physical postures practiced in yoga to promote well-being, flexibility, strength, and balance. Asanas are integral to the practice of yoga.

Ashtanga: An eight-limbed path of yoga outlined in the Yoga Sutras of Patanjali, encompassing ethical guidelines, physical postures, breath control, and meditation techniques.

Aum/Om Symbol: A sacred syllable and spiritual symbol representing the universe's sound in Hinduism, Buddhism, and Jainism, symbolizing the essence of the ultimate reality or consciousness.

Ayurveda: An ancient holistic system of medicine from India, focusing on balancing body, mind, and spirit through lifestyle practices, diet, herbal remedies, and therapeutic treatments.

Babaji (Babaji Cave): A revered immortal yogi associated with sacred meditation caves in the Himalayas, believed to impart spiritual wisdom and guidance to sincere seekers.

Bahá'u'lláh (1817–1892): Founder of the Bahá'í Faith, teaching unity, peace, and justice, and considered a Manifestation of God by Bahá'ís.

Bahai: A follower of the Bahá'í Faith emphasizing unity of all people, religions, and races, and advocating for social justice and equality.

Bhagavan Krishna: Estimated to have lived around 3,000 BCE according to Hindu tradition. Revered as the eighth avatar of the god Vishnu and a central figure in Hindu mythology.

Brahma: A Hindu deity symbolizing creation, knowledge, and creativity, often depicted as a four-headed figure representing the four Vedas.

Bridge pose (Setu Bandha Sarvangasana): A yoga posture lifting the hips while lying on the back, stretching the chest, neck, and spine, and strengthening the legs, buttocks, and back muscles.

Buddha (Approximately 6th to 4th century BCE): Founder of Buddhism, whose teachings form the basis of the religion, emphasizing the Four Noble Truths and the Eightfold Path to enlightenment.

Buddhism: A religion based on the teachings of Buddha, emphasizing enlightenment, compassion, and the cessation of suffering through meditation and ethical living.

Camel pose (Ustrasana): A kneeling yoga posture stretching the chest, abdomen, and thighs, and improving spinal flexibility and posture.

Cat/Cow pose (Chakravakasana): A yoga pose alternately arching and rounding the spine, promoting flexibility and mobility in the spine and relieving tension in the back and neck.

Chakras: Energy centers in the body believed to impact physical, mental, and emotional well-being, associated with specific qualities and located along the spine.

Child's pose (Balasana): A resting yoga posture performed kneeling with the forehead resting on the ground or a prop, promoting relaxation, stress relief, and surrender.

Christianity: A monotheistic religion based on the life and teachings of Jesus Christ, emphasizing love, forgiveness, and salvation through faith in Jesus as the Son of God.

Cobra pose (Bhujangasana): A yoga posture lifting the chest while lying on the stomach, stretching the spine, chest, shoulders, and abdomen, and strengthening the back muscles.

Consciousness: Awareness and perception of surroundings, thoughts, and feelings, considered a fundamental aspect of human existence and spiritual inquiry.

Corpse pose (Savasana): A yoga posture for complete relaxation and integration of the benefits of the practice, typically performed lying on the back with the body in a neutral position.

Dalai Lama: Spiritual leader of Tibetan Buddhism, symbolizing compassion and wisdom, and considered the reincarnation of Avalokiteshvara, the bodhisattva of compassion.

David R. Hawkins: Psychiatrist and spiritual teacher known for his work on consciousness, including the "Map of Consciousness" and the concept of levels of human consciousness.

Dharana: Concentration practice in yoga, focusing the mind on a single point or object to cultivate mental focus and clarity.

DNA: Molecule containing genetic information in living organisms, consisting of two long strands forming a double helix structure.

Donald Walsh: Contemporary spiritual author known for "Conversations with God," a series of books presenting a dialogue between the author and a divine entity, exploring spiritual truths and insights.

Dosha: Biological energies in Ayurveda influencing health, categorized as Vata (air and space), Pitta (fire and water), and Kapha (earth and water), with each person having a unique combination.

Downward-facing dog (Adho Mukha Svanasana): A yoga posture stretching the back, shoulders, hamstrings, and calves, and strengthening the arms and legs, performed by forming an inverted V shape with the body.

Dhyana: Meditation practice in yoga, cultivating deep concentration and awareness to attain inner peace and insight.

Eagle pose (Garudasana): A standing yoga posture involving twisting arms and legs, improving balance, focus, and flexibility, and stretching the shoulders, upper back, hips, and thighs.

Eat Right 4 Your Type: Dietary concept based on blood type by Dr. Peter J. D'Adamo, suggesting that individuals should eat certain foods and avoid others based on their blood type for optimal health.

Eight Limbs of Yoga: Guiding principles in yoga for spiritual growth and self-realization, outlined in Patanjali's Yoga Sutras, encompassing ethical guidelines, physical postures, breath control, and meditation.

Extended Table-top pose (Dandayamana Bharmanasana): A yoga posture for core strengthening, performed on the hands and knees with the spine in a neutral position and the core engaged.

Fibromyalgia: Chronic disorder characterized by widespread pain, fatigue, sleep disturbances, and cognitive difficulties, with the exact cause unknown and treatment focusing on symptom management.

Fish pose (Matsyasana): A yoga posture arching the back and neck, opening the chest and throat, and stretching the hip flexors and intercostal muscles.

Forward bend (Uttanasana): A yoga posture folding the body forward from the hips, stretching the hamstrings, calves, and spine, and promoting relaxation and stress relief.

Four-Part Yogic Breath: A breathing technique in yoga involving inhaling and exhaling through the nostrils in four distinct stages, promoting relaxation, awareness, and concentration.

Garland pose (Malasana): A yoga posture performed in a squatting position, stretching the hips, groin, ankles, and lower back, and improving flexibility and mobility in the lower body.

Guru: A spiritual teacher or guide in Hinduism, Buddhism, and Sikhism, offering wisdom, guidance, and support on the spiritual path.

Halasana (Plow pose): A yoga posture where the practitioner lies on their back and lifts their legs overhead, touching the ground behind them, stretching the spine and shoulders and promoting relaxation.

Hanumanasana (Monkey pose): A yoga posture stretching the thighs, groin, and hamstrings, performed by extending one leg forward and the other backward with the hips squared.

Hatha Yoga: A branch of yoga focusing on physical postures (asanas) and breath control (pranayama) to balance and align the body and mind, preparing for meditation and spiritual practices.

Hinduism: The oldest religion, originating in ancient India and emphasizing concepts such as karma (the law of cause and effect), dharma (duty and righteousness), and moksha (liberation from the cycle of birth and death).

Jesus Christ (Estimated 4 BCE to 30/33 CE): A central figure in Christianity, believed by Christians to be the Son of God and the savior of humanity, whose life and teachings form the basis of the Christian faith.

Judaism: A monotheistic religion of the Jewish people, based on the Torah (the first five books of the Hebrew Bible) and emphasizing the covenant between God and the Jewish people.

Kapha: One of the three doshas in Ayurveda, representing the elements of earth and water, associated with qualities such as stability, calmness, and nourishment, and imbalancccs can lead to lethargy and congestion.

Krishna (Approximately 3228 BCE to 3102 BCE): A Hindu deity, considered an incarnation of Vishnu, known for his role in the Bhagavad Gita and revered as a divine teacher and guide.

Lao Tzu (Approximately 6th century BCE): An ancient Chinese philosopher and founder of Taoism, credited with writing the Tao Te Ching, which emphasizes the Tao (the way), simplicity, and harmony with nature.

Law of Attraction: A metaphysical belief that positive or negative thoughts and intentions attract corresponding experiences or outcomes, popularized by the New Thought movement and the book "The Secret" by Rhonda Byrne.

Law of Cause and Effect (Karma): A fundamental principle in Hinduism, Buddhism, and other Eastern philosophies, stating that every action has consequences, and individuals are responsible for their actions and their effects.

Life Force: A concept in various spiritual and philosophical traditions, representing the vital energy or animating force that sustains life and supports physical, mental, and spiritual well-being.

Lion pose (Simhasana): A yoga posture involving a kneeling position and roaring breath, stretching the face, throat, and neck, releasing tension and promoting relaxation.

Luke 10:27 (Estimated 80–110 CE): A verse from the New Testament of the Bible, where Jesus summarizes the greatest commandments as loving God with all one's heart, soul, strength, and mind, and loving one's neighbor as oneself.

Mahatma Gandhi (1869–1948): A leader of India's independence movement against British rule, known for his philosophy of nonviolent resistance (Satyagraha) and his advocacy for civil rights, equality, and justice.

Mantra: A sacred word, sound, or phrase repeated silently or aloud in meditation, prayer, or ritual practice, believed to have spiritual or transformative power.

Matthew 6:33 (Estimated 70–110 CE): A verse from the New Testament of the Bible, where Jesus encourages seeking first the kingdom of God and His righteousness, with the promise that all other things will be provided.

Metabolism: The process by which the body converts food and nutrients into energy to support cellular functions, growth, and repair, regulated by hormones and influenced by factors such as diet, exercise, and genetics.

Mother Teresa (1910–1997): A Roman Catholic nun and missionary known for her humanitarian work in Kolkata (Calcutta), India, caring for the sick, poor, and marginalized through her Missionaries of Charity organization.

Mountain pose (Tadasana): A foundational standing yoga posture where the practitioner stands tall with feet together, arms relaxed at the sides, and gaze forward, promoting alignment, balance, and groundedness.

Mudra: Symbolic hand gesture or position in yoga, meditation, and Hindu iconography, believed to influence the flow of energy in the body and mind and facilitate spiritual and mental states.

Muscle testing: A technique used in applied kinesiology and holistic health practices to assess the body's response to stimuli by evaluating muscle strength or weakness, often used to identify imbalances or sensitivities.

Muslim: A follower of Islam, a monotheistic religion based on the teachings of the prophet Muhammad, emphasizing submission to the will of Allah (God), and adherence to the Five Pillars of Islam.

Muhammad (Approximately 570–632 CE): The founder of Islam and the final prophet in Islam, believed by Muslims to have received revelations from Allah (God) through the angel Gabriel, which were compiled into the Quran.

Nadi: Energy channels in the subtle body according to yoga and Ayurveda, through which prana (life force) flows, connecting different aspects of the physical, mental, and energetic systems.

Neural pathways: Connections between neurons in the brain that transmit information and facilitate communication within the nervous system, forming the basis of learning, memory, and behavior.

Nikola Tesla (1856–1943): A Serbian-American inventor, electrical engineer, and futurist known for his contributions to the development of alternating current (AC) electrical systems, wireless communication, and other technologies.

Niyama: Ethical observances in yoga, including personal disciplines such as cleanliness (shaucha), contentment (santosha), austerity (tapas), study (svadhyaya), and surrender to the divine (ishvara pranidhana).

Om Symbol: A sacred sound and spiritual icon in Hinduism, Buddhism, and Jainism, representing the essence of the universe and the unity of all creation, used in meditation, prayer, and chanting.

Osteoarthritis: A degenerative joint disease characterized by the breakdown of cartilage in the joints, leading to pain, stiffness, and loss of mobility, typically associated with aging and wear and tear on the joints.

Paramhansa Yogananda (1893–1952): An Indian yogi and spiritual teacher who introduced Kriya Yoga to the West and founded the Self-Realization Fellowship, promoting yoga and meditation for spiritual growth and self-realization.

Patanjali: An ancient sage and the compiler of the Yoga Sutras, foundational texts of classical yoga philosophy, outlining the principles and practices of yoga for spiritual liberation.

Phenomenology: A philosophical approach emphasizing the study of subjective experiences and consciousness, focusing on the first-person perspective and the essence of phenomena as they appear to the individual.

Physical Therapy: Healthcare profession focused on improving mobility, function, and quality of life through movement, exercise, manual therapy, and patient education, often used to treat injuries, illnesses, or disabilities.

Pitta: One of the three doshas in Ayurveda, representing the elements of fire and water, associated with qualities such as digestion, metabolism, and transformation, and imbalances can lead to irritability and inflammation.

Prenatal Yoga: Yoga practiced during pregnancy, focusing on gentle stretches, breathing exercises, and relaxation techniques to support physical comfort, emotional well-being, and preparation for childbirth.

Prithvi: One of the five elements (panchamahabhutas) in Hinduism and Ayurveda, representing the element of earth, associated with stability, grounding, and nourishment, and related to the sense of smell.

Prāṇa: Vital life force or energy in Hindu philosophy and yogic traditions, permeating the body and mind, and influencing physical, mental, and emotional well-being through breath, movement, and meditation practices.

Pranayama: Breath control techniques in yoga, regulating the flow of prana (life force) through conscious manipulation of the breath, promoting relaxation, energy balance, and mental clarity.

Pratyahara: Withdrawal of the senses in yoga, redirecting attention inward and disconnecting from external stimuli to cultivate inner awareness and concentration.

Qi (Chi): Vital energy or life force in traditional Chinese medicine and philosophy, believed to flow through meridians in the body, influencing health, vitality, and well-being.

Qigong (Chi Kung): Ancient Chinese system of movement, breath, and meditation practices designed to cultivate and balance qi (life force), promoting health, vitality, and inner peace.

Rāja Yoga: A path of yoga outlined in Patanjali's Yoga Sutras, emphasizing meditation, concentration, and mental discipline to achieve self-realization and spiritual liberation.

Reiki: Japanese energy healing technique involving the channeling of universal life force energy through the practitioner's hands to promote relaxation, stress reduction, and healing on physical, emotional, and spiritual levels.

Sadhana: Spiritual practice or discipline undertaken with dedication and sincerity to cultivate self-awareness, inner transformation, and connection with the divine.

Sagittarius: The ninth astrological sign of the zodiac, symbolized by the archer and associated with qualities such as optimism, adventure, independence, and philosophical pursuits.

Sagittal Plane: An anatomical plane dividing the body into left and right halves, used to describe movements and positions in relation to this plane, such as flexion, extension, and adduction.

Sanskrit: Ancient Indo-European language of India, used in Hinduism, Buddhism, and Jainism for sacred texts, rituals, and philosophical discourse, and considered the language of yoga.

Sarvāṅgāsana (Shoulder stand): A yoga posture involving balancing on the shoulders with the body vertical, promoting circulation, thyroid function, and relaxation, and stimulating the Vishuddha (throat) chakra.

Satya: Truthfulness and honesty in thought, speech, and action, one of the yamas (ethical guidelines) in yoga, promoting integrity, authenticity, and trustworthiness.

Scorpion pose (Vrischikasana): An advanced yoga posture where the practitioner balances on the forearms with the legs extended overhead, resembling the stance of a scorpion, improving strength, flexibility, and focus.

Self-Realization Fellowship: A spiritual organization founded by Paramhansa Yogananda, teaching Kriya Yoga and promoting meditation, ethical living, and self-realization.

Shavasana: See Corpse pose.

Shiva (Approximately 2000 BCE): A Hindu deity symbolizing destruction, transformation, and regeneration, often depicted as the Lord of Yoga and the cosmic dancer (Nataraja).

Shivananda Yoga: A style of hatha yoga founded by Swami Shivananda and further developed by Swami Vishnudevananda, emphasizing a holistic approach to physical, mental, and spiritual well-being.

Shoulderstand: See Sarvāṅgāsana.

Sikh: A follower of Sikhism founded in the 15th century by Guru Nanak Dev Ji in the Punjab region of South Asia. Sikhism is a monotheistic faith that emphasizes the equality of all humans, service to others, and devotion to one supreme God. Sikhs believe in the teachings of the ten Sikh Gurus, as well as the Guru Granth Sahib, the holy scripture considered the eternal Guru by Sikhs.

Simhasana: See Lion pose.

So Ham: A mantra often used in meditation and breathwork. It is derived from the Sanskrit phrase "So Hum," which translates to "I am that" or "I am that I am." It is used as a contemplative mantra to connect with the universal consciousness.

Soma: In the context of your definition as "Body," soma is a term used in yoga and Ayurveda to refer to the physical body, including its structure, functions, and vitality.

Sufism: A mystical branch of Islam emphasizing inner spiritual experiences, devotion to God, and the cultivation of love, compassion, and wisdom through practices such as meditation, prayer, and music.

Sukhasana (Easy pose): A comfortable seated yoga posture with crossed legs, promoting relaxation, grounding, and stability, often used for meditation and pranayama.

Surya Namaskar (Sun Salutation): A sequence of yoga asanas performed in a flowing sequence, synchronized with the breath, and intended to energize the body, calm the mind, and express gratitude to the sun.

Swadhisthana: The sacral chakra in yoga and Hinduism, located at the lower abdomen and associated with emotions, creativity, pleasure, and sexuality.

Swami Satchidananda (1914–2002): An Indian spiritual teacher and yoga master known for his role in popularizing yoga in the West, founding Integral Yoga and the Yogaville ashram in Virginia, USA.

Swami Sri Yukteswar: Swami Sri Yukteswar Giri was an Indian yogi and guru. He was a disciple of Lahiri Mahasaya and the teacher (aka Guru) of Paramhansa Yogananda, the author of "Autobiography of a Yogi." Swami Sri Yukteswar's teachings focused on the harmony between spiritual and scientific knowledge and the universality of all religions.

Swami Vishnudevananda (1927–1993): A disciple of Swami Sivananda and founder of the International Sivananda Yoga Vedanta Centers, known for spreading the teachings of yoga and Vedanta worldwide.

Tadasana: See Mountain pose.

Tao Te Ching: Ancient Chinese philosophical text attributed to Lao Tzu, containing teachings on Taoism, the way of nature, simplicity, and living in harmony with the Tao (the way).

Taoism: Chinese philosophical and religious tradition emphasizing harmony with nature, balance, simplicity, and living in accordance with the Tao (the way), as outlined in the Tao Te Ching.

Tapas: Discipline, austerity, or self-control in yoga, promoting dedication, perseverance, and transformation on the spiritual path.

Tarot Cards: A deck of cards used for divination, meditation, and self-reflection, featuring archetypal symbols and images representing aspects of the human experience and spiritual journey.

The Bhagavad Gita: A sacred Hindu scripture comprising a conversation between Prince Arjuna and the god Krishna, presenting teachings on duty, righteousness, devotion, and the nature of reality.

The Bible: The sacred text of Christianity, comprising the Old Testament (Hebrew Bible) and the New Testament, containing religious teachings, history, poetry, prophecy, and ethical guidelines.

The Body Ecology Diet: A dietary approach created by Donna Gates which focuses on balancing the gut microbiome, emphasizing whole foods, probiotics, fermented foods, and specific food combining principles to support digestion, immunity, and overall health.

The Paleo Diet: Also known as the Paleolithic Diet or Caveman Diet, is a dietary approach inspired by the presumed diet of early humans. It emphasizes consuming foods that were available to our ancestors, such as lean meats, fish, fruits, vegetables, nuts, and seeds, while excluding processed foods, grains, legumes, and dairy.

The Secret: A self-help book and film by Rhonda Byrne, popularizing the law of attraction and the power of positive thinking to manifest desires and achieve success and happiness.

The Seven Spiritual Laws of Success: A book by Deepak Chopra outlining principles for achieving success and fulfillment in life, based on spiritual laws such as the law of pure potentiality, the law of giving, and the law of karma.

Theta: A brainwave state associated with deep relaxation, meditation, and creativity. It is characterized by slower frequency brainwaves and is often experienced during deep meditation or light sleep.

ThetaHealing: A healing modality and meditation technique created by Vianna Stibal. It involves entering the theta brainwave state and accessing the subconscious mind to identify and shift limiting beliefs, facilitating emotional and physical healing.

The Way of the Pilgrim: An anonymous Russian Orthodox work recounting the spiritual journey of a pilgrim seeking to understand the practice of the Jesus Prayer and achieve inner peace and union with God.

Thich Nhat Hanh (1926–2022): A Vietnamese Zen Buddhist monk, peace activist, and author known for his teachings on mindfulness, compassion, and engaged Buddhism, and his efforts for peace and reconciliation.

Third Eye (Spiritual Eye, Christ Center): Refers to an energy center and spiritual concept in various mystical and esoteric traditions. It is believed to be located in the middle of the forehead, at the point between the eyebrows, and is associated with intuition, concentration, insight, and spiritual vision.

Three Gunas: Qualities or attributes in Hindu philosophy and Ayurveda, representing fundamental aspects of nature and consciousness, categorized as sattva (purity and harmony), rajas (activity and passion), and tamas (inertia and darkness).

Throat Chakra: See Vishuddha.

Tibetan Buddhism: A form of Buddhism practiced in Tibet and other Himalayan regions, blending Mahayana Buddhism with elements of Bon and indigenous Tibetan beliefs and practices.

Triangle pose (Trikonasana): A yoga posture involving stretching the legs wide and reaching one arm down to the shin or the floor while extending the other arm upward, promoting strength, stability, and flexibility.

Trikonasana: See Triangle pose.

Ujjayi Breath: Victorious or ocean breath in yoga, involving slow, deep breathing with a slight constriction of the throat to produce an audible sound, promoting relaxation, concentration, and internal heat.

Upanishads: Ancient Hindu philosophical texts exploring the nature of reality, the self (atman), and the ultimate truth (Brahman), forming the basis of Vedanta philosophy and influencing Hindu spirituality.

Ustrasana: See Camel pose.

Vata: One of the three doshas in Ayurveda, representing the elements of air and space, associated with qualities such as creativity, movement, and vitality, and imbalances can lead to anxiety and instability.

Vedas: Ancient sacred texts of Hinduism comprising hymns, rituals, and philosophical teachings, including the Rigveda, Samaveda, Yajurveda, and Atharvaveda, considered the oldest scriptures of Hinduism.

Vinyasa: Flowing sequences of yoga postures synchronized with the breath, promoting flexibility, strength, and mindfulness, and often used in dynamic styles such as Ashtanga and Vinyasa yoga.

Vipassana: Insight meditation in Buddhism, involving mindfulness of breath, body sensations, thoughts, and emotions to cultivate awareness, wisdom, and liberation from suffering.

Vishuddha: The throat chakra in yoga and Hinduism, located at the throat region and associated with communication, self-expression, creativity, and authenticity.

Vrksasana (Tree pose): A yoga posture involving balancing on one leg with the other foot placed on the inner thigh or calf, promoting stability, concentration, and grounding.

William Shakespeare: An English playwright and poet widely regarded as one of the greatest writers in the English language, known for his works such as "Hamlet," "Romeo and Juliet," and "Macbeth."

Yamas: Ethical guidelines in yoga, including moral disciplines such as non-violence (ahimsa), truthfulness (satya), non-stealing (asteya), moderation (brahmacharya), and non-possessiveness (aparigraha).

Yin Yoga: A slow-paced style of yoga involving passive stretching postures held for extended periods, targeting the connective tissues and promoting relaxation, flexibility, and inner awareness.

Yoga Nidra: A guided meditation and relaxation technique in yoga, leading practitioners into a state of deep relaxation while maintaining awareness and presence, promoting stress reduction and mental clarity.

Yoga Sutras: Ancient philosophical text attributed to Patanjali, outlining the principles and practices of yoga, including ethical guidelines, physical postures, breath control, meditation techniques, and the stages of spiritual liberation.

Yogaville: A spiritual community and retreat center founded by Swami Satchidananda in Virginia, USA, offering yoga and meditation programs, teacher training, and holistic living experiences.

Yogi: A practitioner of yoga, often used to refer to someone who has attained a high level of proficiency or spiritual realization in yoga practice.

Yogananda: See Paramhansa Yogananda.

Zazen: Seated meditation practice in Zen Buddhism, involving sitting in stillness and silence, observing the breath and thoughts, and cultivating mindfulness, concentration, and insight.

Zoroastrianism: One of the world's oldest monotheistic religions, founded by the prophet Zoroaster (Zarathustra), emphasizing the battle between good and evil and the importance of ethical living. Zoroastrianism is believed to have originated in the 6th century BCE.

Assumption of Risk, Release of Liability & Indemnity Agreement

I would like to participate in online and or in-person activities suggested and/or facilitated by "No Pain, All Gain", the book, Casey Hughes, and/or Anke Banderski (herein collectively referred to as "Release Into Bliss"). Release Into Bliss, as defined herein, includes its owners, representatives, employees, affiliates, agents and independent contractors.

I have self-awareness of my body, my health, and my wellbeing. I know participating in activities with Release Into Bliss involves inherent risk and could be helpful or harmful depending on my personal circumstances. I risk personal injury which includes (but is not limited to) irritation, muscle strain and sprains, joint injuries, torn muscles, and back injuries, infection, distress, stroke, heart attack, paralysis, or death. **I FREELY ACCEPT AND FULLY ASSUME THE RISK THAT I CAN GET HURT**, not only in the ways described herein within this book, but also in ways that are unknown and unexpected.

It is my responsibility to determine if any activity proposed by Release Into Bliss is good for me. I will make sure to limit my actions to only those I am comfortable with while closely monitoring for any pain or symptoms of injury. I will not participate in any activity I believe could be harmful to my wellbeing. If Release Into Bliss requests, directs, or assists me to do anything that is potentially harmful, in perception or practice, then I will immediately modify or cease the activity.

In addition to the representations I have made above, I agree as follows:

In full consideration of the above-mentioned risks and in full consideration of the fact that I am willingly and voluntarily participating in activities with Release Into Bliss , I hereby WAIVE, RELEASE, REMISE, and DISCHARGE Release Into Bliss of any and all liability, claims, demands, actions or rights of action, or damages of any kind related to, arising from, or in any way connected with, my participation in Release Into Bliss's recommendations, activities, training or events. I further agree to indemnify, defend and hold harmless Release Into Bliss from any loss, damage, liability or cost, including bodily injury or property damage, that may occur as a result or arising out of my reading "No Pain, All Gain" and any activities or practices suggested therein. Such a waiver and release does not apply to Release Into Bliss's willful misconduct or grossly negligent acts.

ARBITRATION AND GOVERNING LAW. Any controversy or claim arising out of or relating to this contract, or the breach thereof, shall be settled by arbitration administered by the American Arbitration Association under its Commercial Arbitration Rules. The number of arbitrators shall be one. The place of arbitration shall be in the County of San Diego, CA. California law shall apply. Judgment on the award rendered by the arbitrator(s) may be entered in any court having jurisdiction thereof.

SEVERABILITY. I agree that in the event any provision of this agreement, including but not limited to the RELEASE OF LIABILITY, ASSUMPTION OF RISK, AND INDEMNIFICATION provisions, is held or adjudicated to be contrary to any statute or law, or otherwise unenforceable, the remaining provisions of this document shall be enforceable to the fullest extent permitted by law.

I HAVE READ AND UNDERSTAND the foregoing Acknowledgment of Risks and Waiver Agreement, and intend that it be binding on me, my heirs, executors, administrators and assigns, and if I am accepting on behalf of a minor child, I represent and warrant that I am doing so with the consent and approval of the requisite spouse (if any) and I understand that I am acknowledging the risks to said child.

Anke, founder of **Release Into Bliss,** an Alternative & Holistic Health & Wellness Practitioner, believes that anything is possible.

She has been practicing the powerful energy healing modality ThetaHealing® since 2007 and teaching it since 2008.

Anke received her Masters of ThetaHealing in 2013 and the Certificate of Science. She is also a Certified Yoga Teacher, a Passion Map™ Facilitator, a Kriyaban Gurubai of Paramhansa Yogananda, and founder of Theta Yoga.

Anke has produced numerous streaming videos and 3 CDs, Heart Healing Meditations, Chakra Meditations for Humans, and Animals and Theta Yoga.

She is passionately committed to empower you to:

- Live free of physical and emotional pain, struggle and dis-ease through the release of limiting subconscious beliefs and emotions
- Embrace your true Self with complete acceptance
- Discover & live your purpose
- Manifest balanced health
- Live the life you love and deserve!

You deserve to be happy, healthy and fulfilled. No matter how much you have struggled in the past, ***change is possible NOW!***

WEBSITE: www.releaseintobliss.com

EMAIL: Anke@ReleaseIntoBliss.com

FACEBOOK: https://www.facebook.com/anke.banderski

LINKEDIN: https://www.linkedin.com/in/anke-banderski-537a131/

YOUTUBE: https://www.youtube.com/@abanderski

INSTAGRAM: https://www.instagram.com/release_into_bliss/

Client Appreciation

"My days used to be 90% panic and 10% good, now they are 99.9% great and .01% panic. At most I feel a little flutter now and again. I can never thank you enough for all that you have done in helping me!"

Greg Austin, CT

"Theta Healing with Anke Banderski has healed every aspect of my life. She provides a safe, peaceful space and gives divine support, guidance, clearing, and healing. Her theta healing helped me through one of the most challenging times of my life. I am eternally grateful to her and her divine expertise and talent."

Megan A., CA

"For many years I felt stuck. My healing with Anke was the breakthrough I had been praying for. My back pain and fear were released, and I can now clearly hear and trust my heart and the voice within. My life is moving forward with ease and joy, I have found new courage and strength and am soaring in my life. Anke is "the real deal" - heart, mind, and soul!"

Marfil Delgado, NY

"I had everyday pain for almost 2 months that prevented me from concentrating at work and made it difficult to sleep comfortably at night. I found Anke's guiding techniques to be soothing and remarkably simple. I liked the idea of trying a non-invasive technique before turning to more aggressive medical treatments. I'm very grateful to Anke for guiding my healing process."

Dinah, San Diego

"Feedback from our listeners is just amazing! You have a very special gift that has gotten the attention of many coming from all across the world to hear you and want to experience healing guided through you.

Michael, Host of *Journey into the Light* Radio Show

"My entire life has changed, and I credit the main driver to ThetaHealing and the "I'm not good enough" past belief which Anke guided me to release. Alone and miserable for many years, now everything has changed for the better"

Laurie, CA

"Thank you for the wonderful work you do. I can feel that you are a true healer."

Bettina, CA

"5 star review for your Body, Mind, Spirit Renewal retreat at Glen Ivy. Anke has a gift of facilitating healing and I continue to enjoy her gift by listening to her CD's at home. If you have the desire, time and are open to receiving healing...sign up with Anke!"

Jackie D, CA

"Anke's guidance enabled me to experience a great visual connection with the Divine that allowed me to deeply feel and expand the exquisite love that was being poured into me. I also experienced the power of her ThetaHealing applied in a yoga class. In each experience, I felt relaxed, uplifted and joyful. Anke is a gifted practitioner who is committed to helping people heal through realignment. Her honoring and affirming process powerfully guides you back into alignment from wherever you begin, resulting in a positive inner shift that continues to uphold and support you."

Monica D. Traystman, Ph.D., CA

"Truly amazing. Anke teaches that such simple changes in our energy and balance make a big difference."

Erica Fontana, NY

"It's been so nice since I received my Theta healing. I have not been this free of pain in a long time. I did yoga today and found it to be a completely different experience because of it. I feel lighter, and with a relaxed disposition as I go about my day. Accepting "what is" makes for a better experience. Please keep doing your work!"

Shelly, CA

"Anke, I'm so THRILLED to say that ever since I have been meditating through your simple techniques, I no longer suffer from anxiety with panic attacks, depression and health problems I used to have. I feel so free! My life has truly changed for the better. When I first met you I suffered from so many afflictions, and was to the point where I was suicidal. Now I'm living my best life and things continue to get better. My new business is growing and most importantly, I'm growing. I learned how to embrace self-love and I couldn't be any happier. You are a beautiful person with such a beautiful heart."

Diana, CA

"Through Anke's guidance, I have become sensitive to the words and language I use to talk to myself as well as others. If you are contemplating applying the Keys illustrated in "No Pain, All Gain", what do you have to lose? It will only aid everything you're currently doing or show you the way for what's not working."

Brittney Joyce, CA

Made in the USA
Columbia, SC
24 April 2024

34494930R00150